Y'ALL COME BACK, NOW

Y'ALL COME BACK, NOW

Recipes and Memories

Ibbie Ledford

Drawings by Willie Ledford

PELICAN PUBLISHING COMPANY

Gretna 1994

Copyright © 1994
By Ibbie Ledford
All rights reserved

*The word "Pelican" and the depiction of a pelican are trademarks
of Pelican Publishing Company, Inc.,
and are registered in the U.S. Patent and Trademark Office.*

Library of Congress Cataloging-in-Publication Data

Ledford, Ibbie.
  Y'all come back, now : recipes and memories / Ibbie Ledford :
drawings by Willie Ledford.
    p. cm.
  Includes index.
  ISBN 1-56554-015-8
  1. Cookery, American—Southern style. I. Title.
TX715.2.S68L444 1994
641.5975—dc20   93-6074
                                                              CIP

Manufactured in the United States of America

Published by Pelican Publishing Company, Inc.
1101 Monroe Street, Gretna, Louisiana 70053

To my son Tim. I could never have written this book without your help. You're a good son.

To my sister Margaret, who has literally helped me through life.

And to my many relatives and friends for their interest and support. I really appreciate each one of you.

A Tennessee Smoky Mountain Howdy! Photo taken in 1967.

Contents

Introduction 9
Appetizers and Snacks 13
Breads and Beverages 33
Salads, Dressings, and Soups 53
Meats and Main Dishes 69
Vegetables 115
Cakes and Pies 129
Cookies, Candies, and Other Desserts 175
Miscellaneous and How-To 205
Index 215

The family: son Tim, Willie, son Steve and his wife Sharron, daughter Debby, and grandchildren Diedra, Steve Jr., Tray, and Will. I'm sitting on the floor.

Introduction

"Y'all come back" is a common expression of southern hospitality that is sometimes misunderstood by Yankees and people from other areas of the country.

When my brother Chock and his wife Mae moved to Detroit, a neighbor came for a visit. After visiting for a while, Mae walked her to the door. The neighbor had already gotten out to the sidewalk when Mae said, "Come back now, Betty." She came back, talked awhile longer, then started to leave again. When Mae repeated, "Come back, now," Betty walked back and said, "Why do you want me to keep coming back?" May laughed and explained, "I didn't mean for ye to come back right now. I meant for ye to come back to see us when ye ken."

Our small town restaurant, the Dinner Bell, is on the road leading to an automobile parts plant. The food is delicious: homemade rolls, corn bread, pies, and just good southern cooking served cafeteria-style. While visiting the plant, many northern and foreign dignitaries stop in at the Dinner Bell to eat and discuss business. One day, we were eating at a table near a group of Japanese businessmen. They had their briefcases out and were conversing in Japanese. As they paid the check and started out the door, the waitress said, "Y'all come back now, ya hear."

This book contains good simple recipes served with down-home country humor. If you serve your guests food made from the recipes in this book, they will definitely "come back." Interspersed throughout the book are short stories, humorous quips, and tales that I recall hearing over the years. You may also find the stories in Sick Humor—stories of people who use humor to help them endure illness—to be most interesting. It was a pleasure puttin' all this together for y'all, and I sure hope ye enjoy it!

My husband, Willie Ledford waving to friends and saying, "Y'all come back, now."

Y'ALL COME BACK, NOW

Appetizers and Snacks

With Stories from Family and Friends

Green Onion Dip, Popeyes, and Dog Bites.

HELPFUL HINTS

• For an alternative to fatty snacks, wash and prepare fresh vegetables such as celery, cauliflower, or carrots. Place in bags and refrigerate.

CHEESE TARTLETS

8 slices sandwich bread
¾ cup grated Swiss cheese
¼ cup grated parmesan cheese
1 tbsp. fresh minced parsley
1 tsp. Dijon mustard
⅛ tsp. garlic powder
¼ tsp. hot sauce
3 egg whites
2 tbsp. diced pimiento, drained

Remove crust from bread. Cut each slice into four squares. Press each square into a miniature muffin pan. Bake in a 400-degree oven for 3 to 4 minutes. Remove from oven and set aside. Combine next six ingredients and set aside. Beat egg whites until stiff. Fold in cheese mixture. Spoon 1 teaspoon of mixture into each tart shell. Bake in 400-degree oven for 6 to 8 minutes, or until filling is slightly puffed. Garnish with pimiento. Serve hot. *Yields 32 tartlets.*

CREAM CHEESE DIP

This is a hearty dip that can almost serve as a full meal.

1 lb. pork sausage
1 10-oz. can tomatoes and green chilies
2 8-oz. pkg. cream cheese
Bread sticks or tortilla chips

Brown sausage, stirring to break it up as it browns. Drain. Place tomatoes in saucepan over low heat. Add chopped cream cheese. Cook just until cheese melts, about 5 minutes. Process in blender until smooth. Add sausage. Serve with bread sticks or tortilla chips. *Yields 4½ cups.*

CRISPY TUNA BALLS

Cooked chopped chicken or turkey can be substituted for the tuna in this recipe.

> **1 6-oz. can tuna, well drained**
> **½ cup fine dry bread crumbs**
> **2 tbsp. minced onion**
> **2 tbsp. parsley**
> **2 tsp. prepared mustard**
> **3 tbsp. mayonnaise**
> **¼ tsp. liquid hot pepper sauce**
> **1 egg, lightly beaten**
> **3 tbsp. melted margarine**
> **1 cup crushed cornflakes**

Flake tuna with fork. Stir in crumbs, onion, parsley, mustard, mayonnaise, hot pepper sauce, and egg until well blended. Shape into balls, using about 2 teaspoons for each. Dip balls in melted margarine and roll in cornflakes to coat. Place balls 1 inch apart on ungreased baking sheet. Bake uncovered in a 450-degree oven for 8 to 10 minutes, or until hot and crisp. *Yields 2 dozen.*

DOG BITES

> **1 lb. jumbo hot dogs**
> **2 cups ketchup, heated**

Brown hot dogs on barbecue grill, or boil or cook in oven. Cut each hot dog into four pieces. Place pieces in serving dish. Heat ketchup. Pour over hot dog pieces. Stick toothpicks in each piece. Serve hot. *Yields 32 bites.*

DEEP-FRIED CHICKEN PUFFS

Crabmeat or turkey can be used in place of the chicken in this recipe.

> 1½ cups biscuit baking mix
> ⅓ cup grated parmesan cheese
> ¼ cup finely chopped green onion
> 1 cup cooked chicken
> 1 egg
> ⅓ cup water
> 1 tsp. Worcestershire sauce
> ¼ tsp. liquid hot pepper sauce
> **Salad oil**

Stir together biscuit mix, cheese, and onion. Chop chicken and stir into cheese mixture. Set aside. Beat together egg, water, Worcestershire sauce, and hot pepper sauce. Stir into biscuit mixture. Drop batter by teaspoonfuls into hot oil. Cook, turning as necessary, until golden brown on all sides. Lift out with a slotted spoon, and drain on paper towels. Serve warm. *Yields 3 dozen.*

GREEN ONION DIP

> 1 cup salad dressing or mayonnaise
> 1 cup sour cream
> ½ cup chopped green onion
> 1 tsp. Worcestershire sauce
> ⅛ tsp. garlic powder
> **Chips or raw vegetables**

Combine first five ingredients. Mix well. Serve with chips or raw vegetables. *Yields 2½ cups.*

HAM AND CHEESE LOGS

1 cup shredded cheddar cheese
1 8-oz. pkg. cream cheese
1 3-oz. can deviled ham
½ cup chopped ripe olives
½ cup finely chopped pecans
Round butter crackers

Have cheeses at room temperature. Place in mixing bowl. Beat until blended. Add deviled ham and olives. Chill until firm. Shape chilled cheese mixture into two 8-inch logs. Roll logs in pecans. Slice into ¼-inch slices and serve on round butter crackers. *Yields 64.*

HAM AND EGG ROLLS
WITH SOUR CREAM SAUCE

1 3-oz. can deviled ham
2 hard-boiled eggs, chopped
1 tsp. prepared mustard
½ cup crushed potato chips

Combine deviled ham, eggs, and mustard. Chill. Shape into small balls. Just before serving, roll balls in crushed potato chips. Serve on toothpicks to dunk in sour cream sauce. *Yields about 2 dozen.*

SOUR CREAM SAUCE

½ cup sour cream
4 tbsp. ketchup
¼ tsp. salt

Combine all ingredients. Chill. *Yields about ¾ cup.*

PIMIENTO AND CHEESE SPREAD

Pimiento and cheese sandwiches are a big hit at any picnic or gathering.

**2 cups grated American cheese
1 4-oz. jar diced pimiento, drained
1 cup mayonnaise
Bread or celery stalks**

Mix cheese, pimiento, and mayonnaise together. Spread on bread for sandwiches, or use to fill celery stalks. *Yields 3 cups.*

PIZZA TOAST

This is a quick and easy way to get the taste of pizza. Even children can make these by leaving off the sausage and using pepperoni or other cooked meat. Also, meat can be omitted for cheese pizza toast. Toast can be placed in the microwave to melt the cheese; however, the toast will not stay crispy.

**1 lb. pork sausage
8 slices thin sandwich bread
½ cup pizza sauce
2 cups shredded mozzarella cheese
   or 8 cheese slices**

Place pork sausage in skillet. Brown, stirring to break it up as it browns for 5 to 8 minutes. Drain. In toaster, toast bread. Spread toast with pizza sauce. Place on ungreased cookie sheet. Top with sausage and cheese. Place in a 350-degree oven for 10 minutes, or until cheese is melted. *Yields 8 servings.*

POPEYES

2 tsp. dried onion flakes
2 10-oz. pkg. frozen chopped spinach
½ cup sour cream
½ cup mayonnaise
1 tbsp. bacon bits
4 flour tortillas

Add onion flakes to spinach. Cook spinach as directed on package. Squeeze out water and drain thoroughly. Add sour cream, mayonnaise, and bacon bits. Spread mixture evenly over four tortillas. Roll up tortillas. Chill. Cut into 1-inch slices. *Yields about 3 dozen.*

SOUR CREAM SAUSAGE STRIPS

1 cup chopped onion
2 tbsp. margarine
8 oz. sour cream
1 egg, lightly beaten
¼ tsp. salt
1 cup milk
3 cups biscuit baking mix
1 lb. pork sausage

Cook onion in margarine until tender, 2 to 3 minutes. Set aside. Add sour cream to beaten egg. Stir in salt. Set aside. Stir milk into baking mix, then pat batter into a greased 13-by-9-inch pan. Cook pork sausage in skillet until brown, breaking it up as it cooks, 5 to 8 minutes. Drain.

Sprinkle sausage over dough in pan. Combine sour cream mixture and cooked onions. Spread over sausage. Bake at 450 degrees for 20 minutes, or until set and golden brown. Cut into 2-inch strips and serve warm. *Yields about 25 strips.*

SHRIMP COCKTAIL

1 lb. shrimp, cleaned and cooked
½ cup chili sauce or ketchup
½ tsp. prepared horseradish
½ tsp. Worcestershire sauce
¼ tsp. lemon juice
¼ cup finely diced celery

Chill shrimp in refrigerator. Combine remaining ingredients. Mix in shrimp. Serve in sherbet glasses lined with lettuce leaves. *Yields 4 to 6 servings.*

Note: See index for how to clean and cook shrimp.

SPICY MEATBALLS

1 lb. ground beef
1 egg
½ tsp. salt
¼ tsp. black pepper
1 cup bread crumbs
¼ cup chili sauce or ketchup
¼ cup chopped onion
¼ cup chopped celery
¼ cup chopped green pepper
Hot and spicy bottled barbecue sauce

Add beaten egg to ground beef. Mix in all remaining ingredients except barbecue sauce. Shape into 1-inch balls. Brown on all sides in a heavy skillet on medium heat, about 5 minutes. Remove from skillet to serving dish. Heat barbecue sauce. Serve meatballs on toothpicks. Dip in warm sauce. *Yields about 2 dozen.*

SPINACH SQUARES

4 eggs, beaten
1 10-oz. can cream of mushroom soup
2 10-oz. pkg. chopped spinach,
   thawed and well drained
½ cup chopped toasted walnuts
¼ cup minced green onion
1 cup shredded Swiss cheese
¼ cup grated parmesan cheese
1 8-oz. can refrigerated crescent rolls

Combine all ingredients except crescent rolls. Mix well. Unroll crescent rolls, but do not separate. Press dough into bottom of 13-by-9-inch buttered baking pan, pressing seams together. Spread spinach mixture over rolls. Bake at 350 degrees for 40 minutes, or until firm and pick inserted in center comes out clean. Cut into squares. *Yields 12 to 16 servings.*

STUFFED CELERY

1 8-oz. pkg. cream cheese, softened
¼ cup mayonnaise
1 cup chopped nuts
¼ cup chopped parsley
10 celery stalks, cut into 3-inch pieces
Paprika

Combine cream cheese, mayonnaise, nuts, and parsley. Spoon into celery pieces. Sprinkle with paprika. Cover and chill. *Yields about 2½ dozen.*

STUFFED CHERRY TOMATOES

36 small cherry tomatoes
1 8-oz. pkg. cream cheese, softened
1 tbsp. mayonnaise
¼ cup chopped green onion
2 tbsp. fresh minced parsley
¼ tsp. garlic salt

Cut tops from tomatoes. Scoop out pulp and save for soup or other use. Invert tomatoes on paper towels to drain. Mix cream cheese and mayonnaise together until smooth. Add remaining ingredients. Fill tomatoes with mixture. To serve, place on lettuce-lined tray. *Yields 36.*

TOASTED CHEESE APPETIZERS

1 cup shredded sharp cheddar cheese
¼ cup mayonnaise
2 tsp. grated onion
¼ tsp. red pepper
8 slices bread, crust removed

Combine all ingredients except bread. Spread on bread. Roll up jelly-roll fashion. Secure with toothpicks. Place in freezer for 1 hour. Remove from freezer. Slice into thirds. Place on cookie sheet. Bake in a 400-degree oven for 8 to 10 minutes, until light brown. *Yields 24.*

TACO SQUARES

1 cup self-rising flour
¼ cup shortening
¼ cup cold water
½ lb. ground beef
½ cup sour cream
⅓ cup mayonnaise
½ cup shredded cheddar cheese
1 tbsp. chopped onion
2 tomatoes, thinly sliced
½ cup chopped green pepper

Blend together flour and shortening with pastry blender. Add water. Mix until soft dough forms. With floured hands, press into a greased 8-by-8-inch baking pan, pressing dough ½ inch up the sides. Set aside. Place ground beef in skillet. Cook, stirring until meat is brown, 5 to 8 minutes. Remove from heat, drain, and set aside.

Mix sour cream, mayonnaise, cheese, and onion together. Set aside. Spoon ground beef over crust in baking pan. Layer tomato slices and green pepper over meat. Spoon sour cream mixture over all. Bake in 375-degree oven for 25 to 30 minutes, until edges of dough are light brown. *Yields 8 to 10 servings.*

TINY CHEESE QUICHES

FILLING

2 eggs, beaten
½ cup milk
1½ tbsp. melted butter
1 cup shredded cheddar cheese

Combine eggs, milk, butter, and cheese. Set aside.

PASTRY SHELLS

3 tbsp. melted butter
1 egg yolk
3 to 4 tbsp. ice water
1¼ cups self-rising flour
2 tsp. paprika

Add butter, egg yolk, and water to flour. Stir with fork until all flour is moistened. With floured hands, shape dough into 1-inch balls. Place in lightly greased 1¾-inch muffin pans, shaping each ball into a shell. Spoon filling into each shell. Sprinkle with paprika. Bake in a 350-degree oven for 25 minutes, or until set. *Yields 2 dozen.*

ZIPPY CHEESE AND BEEF BALLS

2 3-oz. pkg. cream cheese, softened
1 tsp. horseradish
1 tsp. milk (optional)
¼ cup finely chopped dried beef
½ cup crushed potato chips
½ cup finely chopped fresh parsley

Blend cream cheese and horseradish until smooth. If too stiff, add milk. Add dried beef and potato chips. Chill until stiff. Shape into small balls. Roll in parsley. Serve on toothpicks. *Yields about 2 dozen.*

STORIES

EVERYBODY NEEDS SOMETHING TO LOOK FORWARD TO

    Our neighbor, Mr. Butler, believed in keeping a woman "in her place." His wife and three daughters not only had all the household chores to do, but worked in the fields as well. On Saturday, when everyone else got the day off to go into town, Mrs. Butler and the girls had to stay home and do the washing, ironing, and other chores they didn't have time for during the week.

    Peggy Butler and I became best friends, and I did so much want her to go into town with me on Saturdays. When Peggy asked her dad, he said, "No, you got no business in town."

    We all felt sorry for Mrs. Butler and the three girls. They were treated like slaves. Mama asked Papa to speak to Mr. Butler about the matter. I heard that this was the way Papa approached the subject. He said, "Ray, I know it's none of my business the way you handle

your women folk, but I've noticed you don't ever let 'em go into town. They don't seem to work with the same eagerness as my women folk do."

"Are you sayin' my women folk ain't hard workers?!"

"No, no, Ray, I'm not sayin' that at all! I'm just sayin' if a body has somethin' to look forward to, they take more pride in their work. Let me tell you how I manage my women folk. I let the wife and two of the girls take Friday off to do the wash and ironin'. Then come Saturday, we all go into town. I give the wife and kids a little spendin' money. Sometimes they go to the picture show. We come home, everybody's happy; it makes the wife a lot better bed partner. I guarantee it!"

Mr. Butler tried Papa's suggestion; it worked. The girls talked of nothing else all week. Peggy and I had a good time on Saturday, and Mr. and Mrs. Butler were smiling more. As Papa said, "Everybody needs somethin' to look forward to."

HILLBILLY HUMOR

When Top and Austin moved to Detroit in the forties, they collaborated with each other to see which one could tell the most ridiculous tales about us "hillbillies;" and many of the born-and-raised Yankees of Detroit believed them.

Top told many of his friends that we didn't have telephones; we got up on a hilltop and yodeled to one another. When Top passed away, I traveled to Detroit for the first time, and there met a Yankee lady. She had heard Top's story, and asked if I would yodel for her. I said, "I can yodel, and I can call hogs and milk cows; but I'm not prepared to do either right now."

Since thinking on this, I have wished many times that I had cut loose to yodeling right there in the funeral home. They may have put me away, but Top would have loved it, and it would have been a great tribute to him.

Another story showing our hillbilly sense of humor took place when Austin had a serious operation and long convalescence in a Detroit hospital. He planned to come back to Tennessee until his strength returned. The day he was to check out, someone put a big sign on his door: Shoes for sale. Going home to Tennessee.

EMPTY POCKETS

Papa Ledford and family worked on the farm by the day. After the crops were laid by, the 'maters picked and taters dug, not much work was to be found until cotton picking time. On the first day of cotton picking, Papa Ledford would give his crew a pep talk. He'd say, "Alright youngins, it's been a long time since we've had work. My pockets is empty and we sopped up the last of the gravy this mornin', so le's git out thar and go adder it."

HITS GONNA BE A CAR

Mr. Tatum, a poor sharecropper, had never owned a car. His only transportation was a horse and wagon. When Ben, Mr. Tatum's son, went to work in the saw mill, it was decided that the time was right for the family to purchase a car. Mr. Tatum told Papa, "Old Ben's a gitten us a car."

Papa said, "What kind is he gitten, Mr. Tatum?"

"Wull, I don't rightly know off hand, but hits gonna be a new un or a used un, one er the tuther."

NEW SHOES?

After driving her car through inspection, Ruby was told that the brakes didn't pass. When she asked the attendant what the problem was, he said, "Your brakes didn't pass. I think they need new shoes."

"New shoes?" Ruby exclaimed. "Your kidding me!" But he assured her the brakes on a car contained a part called shoes. She said, "I don't believe this. I have three kids who are always needing shoes, and now you tell me my car needs new shoes?"

THE CON GAME

Papa sold a bale of cotton, settled up with Mr. Rucker, and brought home candy for everyone. Johnnie ate her candy right away, while I still had most of mine left. She asked me to share, and when I refused, she began to flap her arms and open her mouth real big, and say, "Feed the birdie!"

Being only five years old, I thought this was funny, until I had fed her all my candy. When I realized what had happened—that my candy was all gone—I began to cry. Johnnie whispered, "Don't cry! Don't cry! Go get a biscuit from Mama, and I'll act like a birdie again." The game went on until the biscuit was gone and I had forgotten about the candy. A nine-year-old con artist at work!

ANY DETERRENT IS BETTER THAN NONE

My brother, concerned about his daughter and her fiance's plans to make the 300-mile trip to visit us, called and said, "Are you sure you have room for them? You know they will have to have separate bedrooms." I assured him I had plenty of room, would put them in separate bedrooms, and set mouse traps at the doors.

ENOUGH IS ENOUGH

Lois recounts the story of how the family found out about the triplets, her grandchildren. Kimberly went to the doctor. He told her she was pregnant. The next time she went he said she would have twins. On the third visit, he said she was going to have triplets. Lois said, "I told her not to go back to that doctor anymore."

CUSTOMS

After checking the trunk of the car at the Canadian border, the patrol officer came to the window and asked, "Do you have anything to declare?" After they were told to move on, my sister-in-law, a real Southern belle, exclaimed, "I should have said, 'I do dee'-cleah, you sure are nosey.'"

TOO COLD FOR COMFORT

When Chock, a real southern boy, moved to Michigan, he was persuaded to try ice fishing. There were many things he didn't like about the sport, but he said, "The main thing I didn't like was my ice hole kept freezing over."

THE YARD SALE

Willie and Joe went to a yard sale featuring men's clothing. Willie was wearing a nice gray and black plaid sports coat, but pulled it off to try on others. He soon found his bargain, a beautiful Botany 500 suit, for only twenty dollars! With no reason to look further, he began searching for his sports coat, but it was nowhere to be seen. He walked toward the door where the lady was taking in the money just in time to see her fold his coat and put it in a sack: Joe had bought Willie's coat! After a lot of explaining, Willie finally convinced the lady to give him back his coat and return Joe's ten dollars.

Willie came home the proud owner of a great bargain. When he tried the suit on, it was a perfect fit. The style and color were just right. We were thrilled until he turned his back. Then I saw it: a big darned place about the size of a donut right in the seat! I didn't know what to do. Should I be a good wife and stand behind him to let him get at least one good wear out of it? I decided I may not be able to stand close enough to hide the darn, so I told him the bad news. It was quite a blow, and it took him some time to get over it. However, I consoled him by pointing out that patched elbows have been the "in" fashion for several years. Maybe next year it will be darned seats.

A "STUPID" MISTAKE

As Joanie took her walk one morning, the Baxters' dog was in the front yard (again) and ran toward her barking furiously. She crossed the street to avoid him, but he continued barking until she got out of sight. Joanie wondered why the dog wasn't kept in the fenced back yard. On her way back, she noticed the dog was behind the fence, so she decided it was time, while it was safe, to make a complaint.

The den door to the Baxter house was on the side next to the back yard. As Joanie approached the door, the dog began his loud barking. She knocked on the door. Lynn Baxter opened it and Joanie had barely said, "Lynn, you better keep that dog up," when Lynn shouted, "Shut up, Stupid!" This made Joanie so mad that she slapped Lynn. Lynn was so surprised, she gasped, let out a cry, and slammed the door.

Joanie went home and told her husband Herb what happened. He said, "We better go straighten things out." Well, Lynn and her husband, David, were also on their way to "straighten things out."

They met in the street in front of the Baxter house. After much shouting and a shove, the fight was on, the men using their fists and the women throwing shoes and pulling hair. Some of the neighbor men finally got them apart, and they all went home. Each couple called the police and had the other arrested for assault.

My ten-year-old said, "Mama, it all happened because Mrs. Baxter told old Stupid to shut up."

I said, "Son, don't call Mrs. Joanie stupid.

He said, "I'm not calling Mrs. Joanie stupid, Mama. That's the dog's name."

Breads and Beverages

With Stories about
The Country Way

Rolls or bread.

HELPFUL HINTS

• To make yeast breads rise quickly, place in oven with a pan of hot water on the oven rack underneath the bread and close the oven door.

• To use up stale bread, make bread crumbs. Place bread pieces on a cookie sheet. Bake in a 350-degree oven for 15 to 20 minutes, or until crisp and brown. Let cool. Crumble into a blender. Blend to make fine bread crumbs. You can also use crumbled stale bread as stuffing, or sprinkle it on your lawn for the birds.

• Another way to use stale bread is to make salad croutons. Spread bread with softened butter or margarine. Sprinkle with seasonings. Cut into small cubes. Place in a bread pan, just covering the bottom. Bake in a 350-degree oven for 10 minutes. Remove from oven and stir. Return to oven and bake for 10 to 15 minutes longer, or until crispy. Let cool, then place in plastic bags. Keep refrigerated.

• This tip came from a man conducting a tour of the Jack Daniels' distillery: "You can't make good whiskey or good coffee unless you got good water. Water that's got iron in it don't make good whiskey or good coffee. We got good water here."

BREADS

APPLE BUTTER BREAD

½ cup shortening
⅔ cup sugar
3 eggs
1½ cups apple butter
2½ cups self-rising flour
¼ tsp. baking soda
1 cup buttermilk
½ tsp. vanilla
1 cup chopped nuts

Cream together shortening and sugar. Add eggs. Beat until smooth. Stir in apple butter. Set aside. Sift together flour and baking soda. Add alternately with buttermilk to the egg mixture, beginning and ending with flour. Mix in vanilla and nuts. Pour batter into two greased and floured 9-by-5-inch loaf pans. Bake in a 350-degree oven for 40 to 45 minutes, until pick inserted in center comes out clean. Remove from oven and cool in pans for 10 minutes. Turn out on wire rack to cool before slicing. *Yields 2 loaves.*

BANANA BREAD

1 cup sugar
½ cup oil
2 eggs, beaten
1 cup self-rising flour
2 bananas, mashed
1 tsp. vanilla
¼ cup chopped nuts

Mix together sugar and oil. Add beaten eggs. Beat in flour. Add bananas, vanilla, and nuts. Spoon into a greased and floured 9-by-5-inch loaf pan. Bake in a 350-degree oven for 1 hour, or until pick inserted in center comes out clean. *Yields 1 loaf.*

BUTTERMILK BISCUITS

⅓ cup shortening
2 cups self-rising flour
⅛ tsp. baking soda
1 cup buttermilk

Cut shortening into flour using pastry blender. Set aside. Mix soda into buttermilk. Stir into flour mixture. Turn dough out onto floured surface. Dough will be sticky. Knead until smooth. Pat out with hand to about ½-inch thickness. Cut into rounds with biscuit cutter. Bake on greased baking sheet in 450-degree oven until brown, 10 to 15 minutes. *Yields about 1 dozen biscuits.*

COTTAGE CHEESE CORN BREAD

1 cup self-rising cornmeal
1 tbsp. sugar
½ cup buttermilk
1 egg, beaten
½ cup cottage cheese
1 tbsp. margarine
Flour

Combine cornmeal, sugar, buttermilk, egg, and cottage cheese. Melt margarine in heavy ovenproof 9-inch skillet. Sprinkle with flour. Add batter and bake in a 400-degree oven for 20 to 25 minutes, or until golden brown. *Yields 6 to 8 servings.*

EASY SWEET BISCUITS

This makes a great sweet roll for breakfast.

4 tbsp. butter or margarine
¼ cup brown sugar, packed
½ cup chopped pecans
1 can biscuits (10 biscuits)

Grease muffin pans. Melt margarine and mix in sugar. Spoon 1 teaspoon margarine-sugar mixture into each muffin cup. Sprinkle with pecans. Place biscuit on top, pressing down lightly. Bake in a 375-degree oven for 15 minutes, or until biscuits are brown. Remove from oven and cool for 5 minutes. Turn out on cookie sheet. Spoon any excess topping or topping left in muffin cups on biscuits. Serve warm. *Yields 10 sweet biscuits.*

GINGER BREAD

⅓ cup oil
½ cup packed brown sugar
1 egg, beaten
⅔ cup dark molasses
2 cups self-rising flour
½ tsp. baking soda
1 tsp. ginger
½ tsp. cinnamon
¼ tsp. cloves
¾ cup buttermilk
½ tsp. vanilla

Beat together oil and brown sugar. Stir in egg and molasses. Set aside. Sift flour, soda, and spices together. Add flour mixture alternately with buttermilk to sugar mixture, beginning and ending with flour. Stir in vanilla. Pour into a greased and floured 9-inch square baking pan. Bake in a 350-degree oven for 45 to 50 minutes, or until cake tests done with wooden pick. Serve warm. *Yields 8 to 10 servings.*

GLAZED ORANGE BREAD

½ cup butter or margarine, softened
¾ cup sugar
2 eggs, beaten
2 tsp. grated orange rind
2 cups plain flour
2½ tsp. baking powder
1 tsp. salt
¾ cup orange juice
½ cup chopped nuts

Cream butter and gradually add sugar. Add beaten eggs and orange rind. Mix well, then set aside. Combine flour, baking powder, and salt. Add flour mixture to creamed mixture alternately with orange juice, beginning and ending with flour. Stir in nuts. Pour batter into a greased and floured 9-by-5-inch loaf pan. Bake at 350 degrees for 50 to 55 minutes, or until pick inserted in middle comes out clean. Remove from oven and cool in pan for 10 minutes. Remove from pan. Cool completely. Drizzle on glaze. *Makes 1 loaf.*

GLAZE

2½ tsp. orange juice
½ cup sifted confectioners' sugar

Combine juice and sugar. Drizzle over cool loaf.

LEMON BREAD

1 cup softened butter or margarine
1 cup sugar
3 eggs
Grated rind of 1 lemon
9 tbsp. lemon juice
1½ cups flour
1½ tsp. baking powder
1 cup sifted confectioners' sugar

Cream together butter and sugar. Beat in eggs one at a time, beating well after each addition. Add lemon rind and 3 tablespoons of the lemon juice. Set aside. Sift flour with baking powder, then blend into lemon-egg mixture. Pour into a greased and floured 9-by-5-inch loaf pan. Bake in a 350-degree oven for 1 hour, or until wooden pick inserted in center comes out clean. Remove from oven and let stand 10 minutes. Turn out onto serving plate. Combine remaining 6 tablespoons of lemon juice with confectioners' sugar. Spoon glaze over bread. *Makes 1 loaf.*

PARMESAN BREAD

½ cup butter, softened
1 cup parmesan cheese
⅛ tsp. garlic powder
¼ tsp. onion powder
1 loaf French bread

Mix together first four ingredients. Set aside. Slice French bread not quite through to bottom. Pull slices apart just enough to spread mixture on both sides. Wrap in foil. Bake in a 400-degree oven for 15 minutes. *Makes enough spread for 1 large loaf of French bread.*

POPOVERS

6 eggs
2 cups milk
¼ cup plus 2 tbsp. butter, melted
2 cups all-purpose flour
¼ tsp. salt
Vegetable cooking spray

Beat together eggs, milk, and butter with whisk until well blended. Add flour and salt, beating until smooth. Let batter rest at room temperature for 5 minutes to half an hour. Heat oven to 375 degrees.

Spray muffin pans with cooking spray. Dust with flour. Spoon about 3 tablespoons of batter into each section. Bake for 40 minutes. Cut 1-inch slits in tops or sides of popovers to allow steam to escape. Bake an additional 5 minutes. Serve hot. For parties, bake in tiny muffin pans, scoop out center, and fill with chicken salad or ham salad. *Yields about 2 dozen.*

SPICY HUSH PUPPIES

1½ cups self-rising cornmeal
1 tsp. sugar
¼ tsp. baking soda
¼ tsp. cayenne pepper
½ cup chopped green onions
1 egg, beaten
¾ cup buttermilk
Oil (for frying)

Mix all ingredients together except oil. Drop by teaspoonfuls into deep, hot oil to brown. *Makes 3 dozen.*

PRETZEL ROLLS

I created these while attempting to make pretzels, but they turned out so puffy and flavorful that they are now one of my favorite roll recipes.

> **1 pkg. rapid-rise yeast**
> **¼ cup warm water**
> **¼ cup warm buttermilk**
> **2 tbsp. butter, at room temperature**
> **1 egg, beaten**
> **1 tsp. salt**
> **¼ cup sugar**
> **2½ cups flour**
> **1 cup grated sharp cheddar cheese**
> **1 egg yolk, beaten**
> **2 tbsp. water**
> **Coarse salt**

In a mixing bowl, dissolve yeast in warm water. Add buttermilk, butter, egg, salt, and sugar, mixing well. Stir in flour and cheese a little at a time. Turn out onto floured surface. Knead until smooth, about 5 minutes. Place in a greased bowl, turning to grease all sides. Cover with cloth and place in a warm place until doubled in bulk, about 2 hours.

Punch down and knead, dividing dough into twelve pieces. Roll each piece between palms of hands to make a rope about 18 inches long. Shape in a U-shape and cross ends. Lift ends and press to sides of ring. This makes the shape of a pretzel. Place on a greased baking sheet. Set aside. Add 2 tablespoons water to egg yolk. Brush rolls with mixture. Sprinkle with coarse salt. Let rise until double, 45 minutes to 1 hour. Bake in a 375-degree oven 15 to 20 minutes, or until brown. *Yields 12 rolls.*

ROLLS OR BREAD

This recipe is equally good as either rolls or bread.

> **2 pkg. dry yeast**
> **1 cup lukewarm water**
> **2 cups hot water**
> **3 tbsp. shortening**
> **2 tsp. salt**
> **¾ cup sugar**
> **¾ cup dry milk**
> **8 cups flour (or more if needed to make stiff dough)**

Combine yeast and lukewarm water. Set aside. Place hot water in large mixing bowl, then stir in shortening, salt, sugar, and dry milk. Allow to cool to lukewarm. Add yeast mixture and flour a small amount at a time, stirring to combine each time until dough is stiff. Turn out on floured surface and knead until smooth. Place in a very large greased bowl, turning to grease all sides. Let rise until doubled, about 1½ hours.

Punch down, kneading slightly. Let rise again for 1 hour. Punch down. Place on a lightly floured surface. Knead. Roll out to make rolls or place in two greased 9-by-5-inch loaf pans. Let rise again until double, about 1 hour. For rolls, bake in a 375-degree oven for 15 to 20 minutes, until brown. For loaves, bake in a 375-degree oven for 45 minutes to 1 hour, or until done. *Yields 3 dozen rolls or 2 loaves of bread.*

QUICK YEAST ROLLS

1 pkg. rapid-rise yeast
1 tbsp. sugar
¾ cup warm water (110 to 115 degrees)
2½ cups biscuit baking mix

Dissolve yeast and sugar in warm water. Stir in biscuit mix. Turn out onto lightly floured surface. Knead until smooth. Roll out and cut with 2½-inch biscuit cutter. Place in a greased baking pan. Cover with a towel and let rise until doubled, about 45 minutes.

Bake in a 450-degree oven for 10 to 15 minutes, or until golden brown. *Yields about 12 rolls.*

STRAWBERRY BREAD

3 cups all-purpose flour
1 tsp. baking soda
½ tsp. salt
2 tsp. cinnamon
2 cups sugar
3 eggs, beaten
1 cup cooking oil
2 10-oz. pkg. frozen sliced strawberries, thawed

Sift together first five ingredients. Set aside. Combine eggs, oil, and strawberries. Add to dry ingredients. Mix well. Pour batter into two greased and floured 9-by-5-inch loaf pans. Bake at 350 degrees for 1 hour, or until pick inserted in center comes out clean. Remove from oven and let cool in pans for 15 minutes. Loosen from sides with knife. Turn out of pans onto wire rack to cool completely before slicing. *Yields 2 loaves.*

TATER ROLLS

2 ¼-oz. pkg. dry yeast
1½ cups warm water
⅓ cup sugar
2 tsp. salt
2 eggs, beaten
½ cup soft butter or margarine
½ cup cooked mashed potatoes
5½ to 6 cups all-purpose flour

Dissolve yeast in warm water in large mixing bowl. Add sugar and salt. Stir in eggs, butter, mashed potatoes, and about half the flour. Beat with mixer until well mixed. Stir in enough remaining flour to make stiff dough. Turn out on floured surface and knead until smooth. Grease large bowl. Place dough in bowl, turning to grease on all sides. Cover and let rise to double, about 1 hour.

Punch down, knead, and shape into rolls. Place rolls in a greased baking pan. Let rise 1 hour. Bake in a 400-degree oven for 12 to 15 minutes, until brown. Brush tops with melted butter. *Yields about 2 dozen rolls.*

BEVERAGES

CHERRY LEMONADE

2 cups sugar
13 cups water
Rind of 3 lemons
1¼ cups lemon juice
1 6-oz. jar maraschino cherries

Mix sugar, 1 cup water, and lemon rind in saucepan. Bring to a boil and boil for 5 minutes. Remove from heat. Discard lemon rind. Add sugar-water mixture to remaining 12 cups water in a 1-gallon jug. Stir in lemon juice and cherries. Serve over ice. *Yields about 1 gallon.*

EASY BOILED CUSTARD

1 3-oz. pkg. vanilla pudding mix
   (not instant)
1 cup sugar
5 cups milk
3 eggs, separated
1 tsp. vanilla
1 cup whipped cream

In a large heavy pan, combine pudding mix, sugar, and ¼ cup milk. Beat egg yolks and add to pudding mixture. Add remaining milk. Cook over medium heat, stirring often until mixture comes to a full boil, about 10 minutes. Remove from heat. Fold in stiffly beaten egg whites and vanilla. Chill. Serve topped with whipped cream. *Yields about 1½ quarts.*

FALSE KICK PUNCH

This punch is said to taste much like beer. It was served at a Fourth of July reception at my sister's house. The laughter seemed much louder than usual, and everyone said they had a wonderful time. Could it have been the "false kick" from the punch?

> **2 46-oz. cans pineapple juice**
> **½ cup sugar**
> **1 tbsp. almond extract**
> **2 33-oz. bottles ginger ale**

Mix all ingredients, stirring until sugar is dissolved. Serve over ice in stemmed glasses. *Yields about 1 gallon.*

False Kick Punch.

GINGERADE PUNCH

1 6-oz. can frozen orange juice
1 6-oz. can frozen lemonade
1 6-oz. can frozen limeade
6 cups cold water
4 cups ginger ale

Combine all ingredients except ginger ale. Chill. Just before serving, pour in chilled ginger ale. *Yields 2 quarts.*

HOT COCOA MIX

I keep this mix handy in the wintertime. It's a great warm-up drink for my husband when he returns from his daily walk.

3 cups powdered milk or coffee creamer
½ cup cocoa powder
1½ cups sugar, or 2 tbsp. sugar substitute
½ cup cornstarch
¼ tsp. salt

Sift all ingredients together and mix well. Store in covered container. To make each cup of chocolate, place 2 heaping tablespoons of mix in a cup. Pour hot water in and stir to blend. *Yields 14 to 16 cups of hot chocolate.*

GRAPE JUICE CRUSH

2 cups grape juice
1 cup orange juice
¼ cup lemon juice
½ cup sugar
2 cups water
1 qt. ginger ale

Mix fruit juices. Stir in sugar and water. Add ginger ale. Serve immediately in glasses partially filled with crushed ice. *Yields 12 servings.*

ICED TEA

As my family often remarks during the heat of summer, "You jest can't beat good-ole ice tea when you're thirsty."

2 qt. water
1 family-sized tea bag (or 5 regular
  tea bags)
Sugar or sugar substitute

Place 2 cups of the water in small saucepan. Let come to a boil. Remove from heat. Drop in tea bag or bags and cover pan. Let set 5 minutes or longer. Pour into a 2-quart pitcher, rinsing and squeezing tea bag into pitcher with back of spoon. Add enough water to make 2 quarts. Add sugar or sugar substitute to taste. Pour in ice-filled glasses. *Yields 2 quarts.*

NO-SUGAR PUNCH

1 small pkg. cherry Kool-Aid
  with Nutra-Sweet
2 qt. water
1 46-oz. can unsweetened pineapple juice
1 2-liter bottle diet Seven-Up

Mix Kool-Aid, water, and pineapple juice together. Just before serving, add diet Seven-Up. *Yields about 1½ gallons.*

PATIO PUNCH

1 small pkg. cherry Kool-Aid,
  unsweetened
1 small pkg. strawberry Kool-Aid,
  unsweetened
2 cups sugar
4 qt. water
1 6-oz. can frozen orange juice
1 6-oz. can frozen lemonade
1 28-oz. bottle ginger ale

Mix together Kool-Aids, sugar, water, orange juice, and lemonade. Just before serving, add ginger ale. *Makes enough for about 30 punch cups.*

ORANGE SHERBET PUNCH

½ gal. orange sherbet
1 33-oz. bottle ginger ale

Place slightly softened sherbet in punch bowl. Pour ginger ale over top. Chop and stir until creamy enough to serve. Serve immediately. For lime sherbet punch, use lime sherbet instead of orange. *Yields about 25 punch cup servings.*

PINEAPPLE SHERBET PUNCH

1 46-oz. can Fruit Juicy Red Punch
1 46-oz. can pineapple juice
½ gallon pineapple sherbet
1 2-qt. bottle ginger ale

Mix together punch and pineapple juice in punch bowl. Spoon sherbet into juice using large serving spoon. Mix in ginger ale. *Yields about 50 punch cups.*

QUICK CRANBERRY PUNCH

1 6-oz. can frozen lemonade
2 pt. cranberry juice cocktail
2 cups ginger ale

Mix lemonade and cranberry juice cocktail. Just before serving, add ginger ale. Pour over ice. *Yields about 2 quarts.*

STORIES

THE COUNTRY STORE

Uncle Sam and his two boys built the store across the road from his house in 1940. It was just one long room with shelves on one side and a porch on the front. Business was good for many years, and the store became a meeting place for the farmers on rainy days and in the winter when they couldn't work. They sat around on nail kegs, swapped stories, and played checkers on the porch when the weather was warm enough. The large shady yard provided a great place for horseshoe pitching.

After Uncle Sam died, Lewis, his oldest son, and his wife Florence moved in with Aunt Fossie to take care of her and the store. Soon the checker players and domino players were crowding the store. Lewis hated to move the players out, so he built a room just for the games.

Times have changed drastically since 1940. The store cannot compete with the big supermarkets in town, but it is still a gathering

place for the community. The games are still going strong. Bologna, cheese, and crackers still sell good, and Florence makes coldcut sandwiches for farmers and the players. Most of the groceries they sell now are to people who are between trips to the supermarket.

In the early days, Uncle Sam didn't stock milk and eggs. Everyone around had cows that produced all the milk they needed, and hens for their eggs. The store now sells a lot of milk.

When someone in the community needs help, they call the store. The games stop, the men load into a truck, and they go see what they can do to help.

A man and woman from a big city came into the store recently. They had never been in a country store before, but had heard about them and the bologna, cheese, and crackers. When they asked Lewis if they could buy some of that traditional fare for their lunch, he said, "Sure! Pull up a nail keg and eat country-style."

PEOPLE HELPING PEOPLE

In our neck of the woods—Perry County, Tennessee—it's still done the old fashioned way. When someone's house burns or another tragedy occurs, the local musicians donate their time, and the ladies bake cakes and pies for a dance and cake walk at the local schoolhouse. All proceeds go to the unfortunate family. The weekly newspaper prints the event free of charge, and merchants post the coming event with the name of the people and their needs on their windows. If a house burns, they even give the size of clothing needed for each family member. Not only are the money and other gifts helpful, but the very thought of so many people caring and sharing in the misfortune gives hope and encouragement.

Salads, Dressings, and Soups

With Stories from a Kid's Point of View

Spinach Salad and Croutons.

HELPFUL HINTS

• To make a milder mustard, add a little mayonnaise.

• For a hardy salad, add chopped leftover chicken, ham, or beef. Also, add leftover meats to soups and stews.

• Save pickle juice. It can be used as an ingredient in salads and slaws. Also, you can drop boiled eggs into any pickle juice, except sweet pickle juice, to make pickled eggs.

BLACK-EYED PEA SALAD

This is a good dish to serve on New Year's; the tradition being that black-eyed peas bring good luck if eaten on New Year's Day.

- 3 16-oz. cans black-eyed peas, drained
- 1 2-oz. jar pimiento, drained and diced
- ½ cup chopped green onion
- ½ cup red wine vinegar
- 2 tbsp. sugar
- 2 tbsp. oil
- ½ tsp. ground red pepper
- ¼ tsp. salt

Combine peas, pimiento, and green onions. Set aside. Mix together remaining ingredients. Pour over peas. Toss to mix. Cover and chill. Serve in lettuce-lined bowl. *Yields 8 to 10 servings.*

CARROT RAISIN SALAD

- 2 cups shredded raw carrots
- ½ cup raisins
- 1 tbsp. mayonnaise
- 1 tsp. sugar
- 3 tbsp. sour cream

Combine carrots and raisins in mixing bowl. Set aside. Blend mayonnaise, sugar, and sour cream together. Stir into carrots and raisins. Serve on lettuce-lined plates. *Yields 4 servings.*

CHEF'S SALAD

1 cup torn lettuce
½ cup chopped green onion
¼ cup chopped celery
¼ cup shredded carrots
1 cup tomatoes, peeled and chopped
½ cup shredded American cheese
1 cup chopped boiled ham
½ cup croutons
2 hard-boiled eggs

On large plate, layer salad in order given, ending with croutons. Garnish with egg slices. Use salad dressing of your choice. *Yields 1 serving.*

CORKSCREW SALAD

1 cup mayonnaise
¼ cup chopped parsley
1 tsp. dried basil leaves, crushed
¼ tsp. garlic salt
1 8-oz. pkg. mild cheddar cheese, cubed
2 cups broccoli florets
1 cup tricolor corkscrew noodles, cooked and drained
2 tomatoes, cut in thin wedges
2 tsp. bacon bits

Combine mayonnaise, parsley, basil, and garlic salt. Toss with remaining ingredients, except for tomatoes and bacon bits. Line tomatoes around salad plate. Fill center with noodle mixture. Sprinkle with bacon bits. *Yields 6 to 8 servings.*

DRESSING FOR FRUIT SALAD

3 oz. cream cheese, softened
2 tbsp. sugar
¼ cup sour cream
Orange juice or other fruit juice

With electric mixer, beat cream cheese, sugar, and sour cream until smooth. Add enough fruit juice to make the consistency desired. *Yields about 1 cup.*

GREEN AND WHITE SALAD

Florets of 1 bunch fresh broccoli
1 medium head cauliflower
1½ cups chopped celery
1 cup green onion, chopped
1 green pepper, seeded and chopped
1 cup mayonnaise
½ cup sugar
½ cup salad oil
⅓ cup white vinegar
1 tsp. dried mustard
1 tsp. salt

In large salad bowl, coarsely chop broccoli and cauliflower. Add celery, green onion, and green pepper. Mix together mayonnaise and remaining ingredients. Pour over vegetables. Toss to coat. *Yields 8 to 10 servings.*

GREEN PEA SALAD

1 cup sour cream
1 tsp. seasoned salt
¼ tsp. pepper
¼ tsp. garlic powder
2 10-oz. pkg. frozen green peas, thawed
1 chopped tomato
½ cup chopped green onion
Tomato wedges
4 slices cooked crumbled bacon

Combine sour cream, salt, pepper, and garlic powder. Stir in peas, chopped tomatoes, and green onion. Spoon into lettuce-lined bowl. Arrange tomato wedges around sides. Sprinkle bacon on top. *Yields 6 to 8 servings.*

HOT POTATO SALAD

6 medium potatoes
Water
½ tsp. salt
2 hard-boiled eggs, peeled and chopped
1 cup chopped green onions
¼ tsp. black pepper
4 slices bacon
⅓ cup white vinegar

Peel potatoes and cut into cubes. Place in saucepan, cover with water, and add salt. Cook until tender, about 15 minutes. Remove from heat. Drain and add eggs, onions, and pepper. Cook bacon in skillet until crisp. Remove from skillet. Drain on paper towels. Add vinegar to hot bacon drippings. Remove from heat. Pour over potatoes. Crumble bacon and add to potatoes. Toss to mix. *Yields 6 servings.*

HAM SALAD IN A CRUST BOWL

⅔ cup water
¼ cup margarine
1 cup biscuit baking mix
4 eggs
1 10-oz. pkg. frozen green peas
2 cups chopped cooked ham
1 cup shredded cheddar cheese
2 tbsp. chopped onion
¾ cup mayonnaise
1½ tsp. prepared mustard

In saucepan, bring water and margarine to a boil. Remove from heat. Add baking mix. Stir until well mixed. Beat in eggs one at a time, continuing to beat until smooth. Spread in bottom of a greased, 9-inch, deep-dish pie plate. Bake in a 350-degree oven for 35 to 40 minutes, or until puffed and dry in center. Remove from oven and set aside to cool. Rinse peas under cold running water to separate. Drain. Mix with all remaining ingredients. When ready to serve, spoon into crust bowl and cut into serving slices. *Yields 6 servings.*

ORANGE COTTAGE CHEESE SALAD

1 12-oz. carton cottage cheese
1 8-oz. carton whipped topping
1 11-oz. can mandarin oranges, drained
1 20-oz. can crushed pineapple, drained
½ cup chopped walnuts
1 3-oz. pkg. orange gelatin

In a large bowl, mix together cottage cheese and whipped topping. Stir in remaining ingredients. Chill and serve in lettuce-lined bowl. *Yields 8 to 10 servings.*

LEMON-LIME SALAD

1 3-oz. pkg. lemon gelatin
1 3-oz. pkg. lime gelatin
2 cups boiling water
1 cup mayonnaise
1 14-oz. can sweetened condensed milk
1 pt. cottage cheese
1 20-oz. can crushed pineapple
1 cup chopped nuts

Dissolve gelatin in boiling water. Set aside to cool. Do not let it begin to gel. Add remaining ingredients. Pour into a 13-by-9-inch pan. Place in refrigerator for several hours. Cut into squares and serve on salad plate lined with lettuce leaves. *Yields 12 servings.*

MUSTARD POTATO SALAD

6 medium-sized potatoes
Water
½ cup milk
½ tsp. salt
¼ tsp. black pepper
2 hard-boiled eggs, chopped
½ cup chopped onion
3 tbsp. mayonnaise
1 tbsp. mustard
Lettuce leaves

Peel and cube potatoes. Place in a heavy saucepan, cover with water, and cook for 15 to 20 minutes, until potatoes are soft. Remove from heat. Drain. Mash and beat until smooth. Add milk, salt, and pepper. Mix until creamy. Stir in eggs and onion. Set aside. Mix mayonnaise and mustard together. Stir into potatoes. Line salad bowl with lettuce leaves. Spoon in potatoes. Serve warm or cold. *Yields 6 servings.*

PEAR SALAD

This is so quick and easy and pretty; however, be sure to add the cherries just before serving to prevent them from bleeding on the cottage cheese.

1 16-oz. can pear halves, drained
1 cup cottage cheese
1 small jar maraschino cherries

Place a pear half on each lettuce-lined salad plate. Spoon on cottage cheese. Top with a cherry. Peach halves may be substituted to make a peach salad. *Yields about 6 servings.*

SPINACH SALAD

⅔ cup salad oil
½ cup wine vinegar
2 tsp. soy sauce
1 tsp. sugar
1 tsp. dry mustard
½ tsp. salt
½ tsp. garlic salt
3 bunches fresh spinach
4 chopped green onions
½ lb. bacon, fried and crumbled
4 hard-boiled eggs, peeled and quartered

Combine first seven ingredients in a pint jar. Shake to mix well. Chill. Wash spinach and tear into bite-sized pieces. Place in salad bowl. Add green onions. Sprinkle with bacon and salad dressing. Toss to mix. Garnish with egg quarters. *Yields 8 servings.*

SPLIT-PEA SOUP

1½ cups quick-cooking split green peas
1 qt. water
2 lb. fully cooked ham shank
1 cup chopped onion
½ cup shredded carrot
½ cup chopped celery
¼ cup chopped parsley
½ tsp. salt (or to taste)
⅛ tsp. pepper
1 13¼-oz. can chicken broth

In a large kettle, combine peas and 1 quart of water. Bring to a boil. Reduce heat. Cover and simmer 45 minutes, adding more water if needed. Add ham and remaining ingredients. Cover and simmer for 1½ hours. Remove from heat. Remove ham shank from soup. Cool and cut ham from bone. Press vegetables and liquid through coarse sieve. Return to kettle with ham. Cook 15 minutes more. Taste and add more salt if needed. *Yields 6 to 8 servings.*

NO-SUGAR SALAD DRESSING

⅓ cup ketchup
⅓ cup red wine vinegar
⅓ cup salad oil
1 envelope sugar substitute

Blend all ingredients together. Serve over salad greens. *Yields 1 cup.*

THOUSAND ISLAND DRESSING

I keep this salad dressing in the refrigerator at all times. My family loves it.

   1 qt. mayonnaise
   1 24-oz. bottle ketchup
   2 boiled eggs, peeled and grated
   ¼ cup onion, grated
   ½ cup sweet pickle relish

Blend mayonnaise and ketchup together. Stir in eggs, onion, and relish. Keep refrigerated. *Yields 3½ pints.*

TWO-BY-TWO FRUIT SALAD

   2 peaches
   2 apples
   2 pears
   2 navel oranges
   2 bananas
   2 cups seedless grapes
   2 8-oz. cartons plain or fruit yogurt

Peel and chop peaches, apples, pears, and oranges. Peel and slice bananas. In a large bowl, mix all together with the grapes and yogurt. *Yields 10 to 12 servings.*

HONEY OF A DRESSING

   1 cup salad dressing
   2 tbsp. honey
   1 tbsp. orange juice or lemon juice

Combine all ingredients. Chill and serve over fruit for a delicious fruit salad. *Yields about 1 cup.*

STORIES

DADDIES, WATCH YOUR STEP

I had dressed my two-year-old in one of his cutest outfits for a trip to town. As we started to get into the car, we both noticed a mud hole nearby. Before I could stop him, he ran over and jumped right into the middle of that mud hole! The water and mud went over his shoe tops and splashed all over his pants. I grabbed him up and demanded, "Why did you do that, Steve?"

He shrugged his little shoulders and said, "That's the way my daddy do."

So Daddies, watch your step as you go through life. Someone may be watching.

DEEP THOUGHTS

Our four-year-old, born a real cotton top, admired his dad's black hair very much. He asked me if his hair would ever be black like his dad's. I told him that as he got older his hair would get darker, maybe even be black.

One day he was sitting in his daddy's lap, lovingly running his fingers through his dad's graying hair, when he said, "You know what, Daddy? By the time my hair gets black, yours will be white."

LOVE CONQUERS ALL

While our four-year-old, Steve, and his friends were playing, little Mike came in crying, "Steve hit me!" When I called Steve in to reprimand him for hitting Mike, Steve put his arm around Mike and said, "It was only a lub lick, Mike."

Mike immediately stopped crying, smiled, and said, "I didn't know dat, Steve." Problem solved, they went back out to play with their arms around each other.

BE CAREFUL—YOU MAY BE A FASHION SETTER

I had just paid an outrageous price for a Western belt with my son's name on it "because everybody else has one." As Steve and his friend Don started off to school one morning, I noticed that both boys were dressed neat with their shirt tails tucked in their jeans, but neither one had on a belt. I said, "Hey, you boys forgot to put on your belts!"

Steve said, "Oh Mama, nobody wears belts anymore."

I was so exasperated, I said, "I'd just like to know who started that fad?" Don answered, "I guess I did, 'cause I don't have one to wear."

JUST BE QUIET!

Little three-year-old Steve had been very rowdy and loud at the library. I had heard a prominent child psychologist say that if a child was told something was a rule, he would usually obey. I decided to try this method on little Steve. When we got home, I sat him down and explained that the library was a place for reading, and they had a rule that everyone was to be very quiet so as not to disturb people who were reading. "Now remember this rule the next time we go to the library," I said.

He looked at me and asked, "Granny, what's a rule?"

WOULD YOU HAVE AN ANSWER FOR THIS ONE?

After my three-year-old grandson's first time in story hour at the library, he said, "Granny, you'll have to take me to story hour every time, so I can learn everything. How long will it take me to learn everything?"

ATTENTION GETTER

Having just bought some eye shadow, the fashion rage of the sixties, I applied just a touch of green to each eye to match the green dress I was wearing to church. The class of nine-year-olds I taught seemed especially attentive that morning. Kathy, whose attention it was usually difficult to hold for very long, sat on the front row, chin in hand, staring at me all through the lesson. I thought, "Great. I'm really getting through to Kathy this time."

After the lesson was over, I asked if there were any questions. Kathy's hand shot up right away. I was very pleased, expecting a question on the lesson. I said, "Yes, Kathy?"

She asked, "Mrs. Ledford, what's that green stuff you've got on your eyes?"

WHAT A SALES PITCH!

The doorbell rang. It was Little Judy from across the street. She said, "Mrs. Ledford, do you want to buy a calendar?"

I said, "We already have several calendars, Judy."

"But we're sellin' 'em so our class can go on a trip before school is out this spring. We're startin' early cause we gonna have to sell lots of stuff to get enough money. If you already have a calendar, you don't have to buy one. I won't get mad or cry or anything."

I bought the calendar.

COMPLETE SATISFACTION

The wedding was very elaborate, with a ring bearer and several attendants. While the ceremony was in progress, I noticed the little ring bearer wiggling and squirming. He placed the pillow with the ring on it in his left hand and tried to scratch his backside. He could not quite reach the place he was aiming for, so he changed hands, encircling the pillow with his right hand and arm. He still couldn't get the results he wanted. He walked over, laid the pillow down on the front pew, and proceeded to scratch exactly where it itched. Finally satisfied, he picked up the pillow, took his place, and waited patiently until the ceremony was over.

THAT OUGHT TO DO IT

Little seven-year-old Jeana said that when she got married, she was only going to have one kid, then have her kidneys tied.

Meats and Main Dishes

With My Thoughts and Stories

Round Steak and Onion Gravy, Green Beans Almondine, Rolls or Bread, Potatoes JoAnn, Spinach Salad, and Apple Rings.

HELPFUL HINTS

• Use Kitchen Bouquet for a browner gravy. It not only seasons the gravy, but makes it look tastier.

• Use self-rising flour to dredge anything for frying. The rising ingredients in the flour make for a puffier crust than plain flour.

• Use leftover meat for a pot pie, or make hash out of leftover chopped beef, chopped potatoes, and leftover gravy. Of course, leftover meat is great for sandwiches.

• Have one night a week as "Leftover Night."

• To prevent fried foods, such as fish and chicken, from becoming soggy, drain in a colander or wire basket for at least five minutes, then place on paper towels to further drain.

• Use lemon juice on hands to remove fish odors.

BASIC WHITE SAUCE

1 tbsp. butter or margarine
1 tbsp. flour
½ tsp. salt
⅛ tsp. pepper
1 cup milk

Melt butter in saucepan. Stir in flour, salt, and pepper. Slowly add milk. Cook, stirring constantly until desired thickness is achieved. For medium sauce, use 2 tablespoons butter and 2 tablespoons flour. For thick sauce, use 3 tablespoons butter and 3 tablespoons flour. *Yields a little over 1 cup.*

Note: Many ingredients can be added to this sauce for different tastes and dishes. For a cheese sauce, just add 1 cup shredded cheese. Onion, celery, parsley, and garlic may be added to butter and sautéed before adding the flour for a different taste. If a creamier sauce is desired, substitute half-and-half or light cream for milk.

BEEF AND RICE CASSEROLE

1 lb. ground beef
½ cup chopped onion
½ tsp. salt
¼ tsp. pepper
2 15-oz. cans pinto beans, drained
2 cups cooked rice
2 16-oz. cans tomatoes, chopped
1 cup sharp cheddar cheese

In a skillet, brown ground beef and onions for 8 to 10 minutes. Drain. Spoon into a 2-quart casserole. Add salt, pepper, beans, rice, and tomatoes. Bake in a 350-degree oven for 20 minutes. Remove from oven and sprinkle top with cheese. Return to oven for 10 minutes, or until cheese is melted. *Yields 8 to 10 servings.*

BEEF STROGANOFF

2 to 3 lb. beef sirloin
Meat tenderizer
4 tbsp. butter or margarine
1 large onion
½ lb. fresh mushrooms, sliced
2 tsp. tomato paste
3 tbsp. flour
2 cups beef broth
½ tsp. salt (or to taste)
¼ tsp. pepper
1 cup sour cream
Cooked noodles or rice

Sprinkle sirloin with meat tenderizer. Cut into strips. Brown in 2 tablespoons of the butter in a heavy skillet for 5 to 8 minutes. Remove meat to 2-quart casserole dish. Set aside. Add remaining butter to skillet. Place skillet back on heat, and stir in onions and mushrooms. Cook until tender, 3 to 5 minutes. Stir in tomato paste. Set aside.

Make a smooth paste of flour and 1 cup of beef broth. Add this along with remaining broth and salt and pepper to onions, stirring until mixture comes to a boil and thickens, about 5 minutes. Gradually add sour cream, stirring until smooth. Remove from heat and add to meat. Bake in a 375-degree oven for 20 minutes. Serve with noodles or rice. *Yields 8 to 10 servings.*

BEEFY CORN BAKE

1 cup self-rising cornmeal
2 cups water
1 lb. ground beef
½ cup chopped onion
½ cup chopped green pepper
1 tsp. flour
1 16-oz. can tomatoes, chopped
1 17-oz. can whole-kernel corn, drained
½ tsp. garlic salt
1 tsp. chili powder
½ tsp. salt
½ cup shredded cheddar cheese

Combine cornmeal and water in a heavy saucepan. Cook and stir over medium heat for 8 to 10 minutes, until thick. Butter a 2-quart casserole dish. Line bottom and sides with cornmeal mixture. Set aside. Brown ground beef, onion, and pepper in skillet for 8 to 10 minutes. Remove from heat, drain, and return to skillet. Blend in flour, tomatoes, corn, garlic salt, chili powder, and salt. Simmer for 5 minutes. Pour into cornmeal shell. Bake uncovered in a 350-degree oven for 25 minutes. Sprinkle with cheese. Return to oven for 5 minutes to melt cheese. *Yields 8 to 10 servings.*

BROILER HOT DOGS

1 lb. hot dogs
1 pkg. hot dog buns
1 cup chopped onions
1 cup grated cheddar cheese

Place hot dogs under broiler until brown, about 5 minutes. Split hot dogs lengthwise. Place on buns. Fill split with chopped onion and cheese. Place back under broiler for about 3 minutes, until cheese melts. *Yields 8 servings.*

BREAKFAST PIZZA

1 lb. hot pork sausage
1 8-oz. can refrigerated crescent rolls
2 cups frozen shredded hash brown potatoes, thawed
1 cup shredded cheddar cheese
6 eggs
¼ cup milk
½ tsp. salt
⅛ tsp. black pepper
½ cup grated parmesan cheese

Cook sausage in skillet until brown, stirring to break it apart as it cooks, 5 to 8 minutes. Remove from heat. Drain and set aside. Separate rolls into 8 triangles. Place on an ungreased 12-inch pizza pan, points toward center. Press together over bottom and up sides to form crust. Spoon sausage over crust and sprinkle with potatoes and cheddar cheese. Set aside. Beat eggs. Add milk, salt, and pepper. Pour over sausage and cheese. Sprinkle with parmesan. Bake in a 350-degree oven for 25 to 30 minutes, until eggs are set. *Yields 8 servings.*

BRUNCH CASSEROLE

2 tbsp. butter, softened
6 bread slices, crust removed
1 lb. pork sausage
1 4-oz. can chopped green chilies
2 cups shredded cheddar cheese
1 cup sour cream
12 eggs, beaten

Spread butter on one side of each bread slice. Place buttered sides down in a 13-by-9-inch baking pan. Place sausage in skillet. Cook sausage until brown, stirring to crumble as it cooks for 5 to 8 minutes. Remove from heat and drain. Layer half of sausage, chilies, and cheese over bread. Set aside. Combine sour cream and eggs. Pour over casserole. Repeat layers of sausage, chilies, and cheese. Cover and refrigerate for about 6 hours or overnight.

Remove from refrigerator and let stand at room temperature for 30 minutes. Bake in a 350-degree oven for 35 to 40 minutes. Cut into squares. *Yields 12 servings.*

THE CAPTAIN'S FISH BATTER

1 cup all-purpose flour
2 tsp. baking powder
½ tsp. salt
¼ tsp. pepper
¼ tsp. paprika
1 cup cold water
1 egg, beaten
Fish fillets

Combine first five ingredients, then add cold water and beaten egg. Beat until smooth. Put fish fillets into batter. Drop one at a time into hot oil. Batter will puff up and become very crispy while fish is moist and tasty inside. *Makes enough batter for 2 pounds of fish fillets.*

CHEESE AND BACON OMELET

>4 slices bacon
>4 eggs
>¼ cup water
>½ tsp. salt
>Dash pepper
>Nonstick cooking spray
>¼ cup shredded cheddar cheese

Cook bacon until crisp. Crumble. Set aside. Combine eggs, water, salt, and pepper. Spray a 10-inch skillet with nonstick cooking spray. Pour egg mixture into heated skillet. As mix cooks, lift and tilt pan. When set and no longer runs, sprinkle with bacon bits and cheese. Fold over and serve. *Yields 2 to 4 servings.*

CHICKEN AND BROCCOLI CASSEROLE

>6 chicken breast halves
>1 tsp. salt
>Water
>3 10-oz. pkg. frozen broccoli spears
>2 8-oz. pkg. cream cheese, softened
>2 cups milk
>1 tsp. salt
>¼ tsp. garlic salt
>½ cup parmesan cheese

Place chicken breasts in saucepan. Sprinkle with 1 teaspoon salt. Cover with water. Cook until tender, about 30 minutes. Remove from broth and discard bones and skin. Set aside.

Cook broccoli according to directions on package. Drain and place in a 3-quart buttered casserole dish. Lay chicken on top. In a heavy saucepan, mix cream cheese, milk, salt, and garlic salt. Stir over medium heat for 8 to 10 minutes, until blended and thickened. Remove from heat. Mix in parmesan cheese. Pour over chicken. Bake in a 350-degree oven for 35 to 40 minutes, or until bubbly. *Yields 6 servings.*

CHICKEN AND RICE IN TOMATO SAUCE

1 lb. skinned and boned chicken,
  cut into strips
½ cup chopped onions
1 green pepper, cut into strips
2 tbsp. butter or margarine
1 28-oz. can tomatoes
1 8-oz. can tomato sauce
½ tsp. dried oregano leaves
½ tsp. dried basil
½ tsp. salt
1½ cups uncooked minute rice

Sauté chicken, onion, and pepper in butter. Add tomatoes, tomato sauce, and seasonings. Bring to a full boil. Simmer for 10 minutes. Stir in rice. Cover and remove from heat. Let stand 5 minutes before serving. *Yields 8 servings.*

CHICKEN GUMBO

1 frying-sized chicken, about 3 lb.
1 qt. water
1 tsp. salt
¼ tsp. black pepper
4 cups sliced okra
1 16-oz. can tomatoes, chopped
2 tsp. dried onion flakes
1 tsp. sugar
Cooked rice

Cut chicken into serving pieces. Place in dutch oven. Add water and salt. Bring to a boil. Reduce heat. Cover pot and simmer until chicken is tender, about 1 hour. Remove chicken from broth. When cool, pull chicken from bones, discarding bones and skin. Skim excess fat from broth. Add to broth the pepper, okra, tomatoes, onion flakes, and sugar. Mix well. Return chicken to mixture. Cover and simmer for 20 minutes, stirring occasionally. Taste to see if more salt is needed. Serve over rice. *Yields 8 to 10 servings.*

CHICKEN IN A NEST

1 12-oz. pkg. slender egg noodles
2 tbsp. butter or margarine
½ cup chopped onion
1 cup chopped celery
½ cup chopped green pepper
1 10-oz. can cream of chicken soup
1 6-oz. can evaporated milk
1 cup shredded American cheese
2 cups cooked chicken, chopped
½ cup bread crumbs
1 tbsp. butter or margarine
½ cup slivered almonds

Cook noodles according to package directions. Drain and form into a nest in a buttered 2-quart casserole. Melt 2 tablespoons butter in skillet. Add onion, celery, and green pepper. Cook until crisp tender, but not brown, about 3 minutes. Mix in soup, milk, cheese, and chicken. Pour into nest. Set aside. Melt 1 tablespoon butter. Add bread crumbs. Sprinkle over chicken mixture, then sprinkle almonds over all. Bake in a 350-degree oven for about 25 minutes, until bubbly hot. *Yields 6 to 8 servings.*

CHICKEN PARMESAN

4 half chicken breasts
½ tsp. salt
2 14½-oz. cans tomatoes, chopped
2 tbsp. cornstarch
½ tsp. crushed basil
¼ tsp. hot pepper sauce
¼ cup parmesan cheese

Place chicken in baking dish. Sprinkle with salt. Set aside. In a heavy saucepan, combine tomatoes, cornstarch, basil, and pepper sauce. Cook, stirring until sauce thickens, about 5 minutes. Pour over chicken. Top with cheese. Cover and bake in a 350-degree oven for 1 hour. *Yields 4 servings.*

CHICKEN OR TURKEY A LA KING

This is a good way to use up leftover turkey.

4 tbsp. butter or margarine
½ cup chopped celery
2 tbsp. flour
1 cup chicken broth
½ cup heavy cream
1 cup green peas, well drained
2 cups chopped cooked turkey or chicken
½ tsp. salt
6 toast points
¼ tsp. paprika

Place 2 tablespoons butter in heavy skillet. Add celery. Cook until celery is tender, about 3 minutes. Mix in flour, stirring to mix well, and cook for about 2 minutes. Add chicken broth and cream. Continue to stir and cook over low heat until mixture thickens, about 5 minutes. Add peas, chicken or turkey, the remaining 2 tablespoons butter, and salt. Cook, stirring constantly, until heated through, about 2 minutes longer. Remove from heat. Serve on toast points. Sprinkle with paprika. *Yields 6 servings.*

CHILI CHICKEN

1 lb. boneless chicken breasts
2 tbsp. cooking oil
1 cup chopped green pepper
1 cup chopped onion
1 28-oz. can tomatoes, chopped
1 tbsp. chili powder
½ tsp. cumin
½ tsp. salt
⅛ tsp. red cayenne pepper

Cut chicken into bite-sized pieces. Cook in oil until light brown, about 5 minutes. Add green pepper and onion. Stir together and let cook for about 5 minutes more, stirring often. Add tomatoes and remaining ingredients. Let come to a boil. Reduce heat and let simmer for 20 minutes, stirring occasionally. Serve in bowls. *Yields 4 to 6 servings.*

CHILI DOGS

1 lb. hot dogs
1 15-oz. can chili, with or without beans
  (or homemade chili)
1 pkg. hot dog buns
1 cup chopped onions
1 cup shredded cheddar cheese

Heat hot dogs in microwave or boil them for about 5 minutes, just until heated. Remove from heat and drain. Set aside. Heat chili. Place hot dogs in buns. Spoon chili over hot dogs. Sprinkle with onions and cheese. *Yields 8 servings.*

CORNY DOGS

6 hot dogs
1 egg, beaten
1 17-oz. can whole-kernel corn, drained
1 17-oz. can cream-style corn
1 cup milk
1 cup shredded Swiss cheese
½ cup herb-seasoned stuffing mix
1 tbsp. chopped pimiento
⅛ tsp. black pepper

Cut hot dogs into 1-inch pieces. Set aside. Combine beaten egg, corn, milk, ¾ cup cheese, stuffing mix, pimiento, and pepper. Stir in hot dogs. Pour into a 1½-quart casserole. Bake in a 350-degree oven for 40 minutes. Top with remaining cheese. Bake 5 additional minutes to melt cheese. *Yields 6 servings.*

CREAMY NOODLES

1 8-oz. pkg. slender egg noodles
6 tbsp. butter, melted
½ cup grated parmesan cheese
½ tsp. dried basil
½ cup sour cream
½ cup whipping cream

Cook noodles according to directions. Drain. Place in serving dish and add butter, parmesan cheese, and basil. Set aside. Gently blend together sour cream and whipping cream. Fold into noodles. Serve while warm. *Yields 6 to 8 servings.*

CREPE CUPS

CREPES

3 eggs, slightly beaten
1 cup milk
⅔ cup flour
½ tsp. salt
Nonstick cooking spray

Combine eggs, milk, flour, and salt. Beat until smooth. Spray an 8-inch skillet with nonstick cooking spray. Place skillet on high heat. Pour 2 tablespoons batter into hot skillet. Cook on one side only, until underside is light brown, about 2 to 3 minutes. Remove from skillet and fit into greased muffin pans. They will be too large and will flower out over the top, but do not trim. Set aside and make filling.

FILLING

1½ cups shredded sharp cheddar cheese
3 tbsp. flour
3 eggs, beaten
⅔ cup mayonnaise
1 10-oz. pkg. frozen chopped spinach, thawed and drained
1 4-oz. can mushrooms, drained
6 crisply cooked bacon slices, crumbled
¼ tsp. salt
Dash black pepper

Toss cheese with flour. Add remaining ingredients. Mix well. Spoon into crêpes. Bake at 350 degrees for 40 minutes, or until set. *Yields 12 crêpes.*

DUKLES
(Spaghetti and Meatballs)

I don't know why, but my sister Margaret's kids always called this dish "Dukles." This is her recipe.

**1½ lb. ground chuck
1 cup chopped onion
2 16-oz. cans tomatoes, blended
   in blender until smooth
¼ cup soy sauce
1 tbsp. sugar
¼ tsp. salt
¼ tsp. pepper
1 tsp. dried basil leaves
½ tsp. dried oregano leaves
1 12-oz. pkg. spaghetti, cooked and drained**

Shape ground chuck into 1-inch balls. Place in a large dutch oven with chopped onion. Brown over medium heat for 5 to 8 minutes. Mix in remaining ingredients, except spaghetti. Cover and simmer 2 hours or more, stirring every 15 or 20 minutes. Add spaghetti. Simmer another 20 minutes, stirring occasionally. Serve hot. *Yields 8 servings.*

EASY BARBECUED PORK

3 lb. pork roast
¾ cup bottled barbecue sauce
½ cup ketchup
1 tbsp. brown sugar
1 tbsp. mustard
2 tsp. hot pepper sauce
1 tbsp. dried onion flakes
½ cup juice drippings from roast

Cook pork roast in crock-pot until very tender. Remove bone, gristle, and most of the fat. Chop meat. Mix together meat and rest of ingredients in a large skillet or dutch oven. Simmer on low heat for about 10 minutes, until heated through and well mixed. Serve on hamburger buns. *Yields 10 to 12 sandwiches.*

Note: I like to put just enough of this meat for one sandwich in small freezer bags and freeze them. It only takes a minute or two to warm up in the microwave, and you have a delicious sandwich any time you feel like it.

EASY CHILI CHICKEN

1 fryer chicken, cut into serving pieces
1 pkg. chili seasoning mix
¼ cup vinegar
Aluminum foil
Salt

Wash chicken and drain. Set aside. Combine chili mix and vinegar. Sprinkle chicken pieces with salt. Using a pastry brush, paint each piece with chili mixture. Place on large piece of aluminum foil. Fold over and seal tightly. Place on baking sheet. Bake in a 400-degree oven for about 1 hour, or until chicken is tender. *Yields about 6 to 8 servings.*

EASY MEATBALL STEW

1 lb. ground beef
½ tsp. salt
¼ tsp. black pepper
1 10½-oz. can onion soup
1 can water
3 medium-sized potatoes,
   peeled and chopped coarse
3 carrots, sliced

Mix together ground beef, salt, and pepper. Shape into small balls. Brown in a dutch oven for 5 to 8 minutes. Remove from heat. Drain off fat. Add soup, water, potatoes, and carrots. Simmer with lid on about 20 minutes, until vegetables are tender, adding more water if needed. Remove from heat. Good served with crackers or corn bread. *Yields 6 servings.*

FRIED STEAKS AND CREAM GRAVY

4 minute steaks or pork steaks
Salt and pepper, to taste
1 egg, beaten
1½ cups milk
1 cup plus 2 tbsp. flour
½ cup oil

Sprinkle meat with salt and pepper. Set aside. Mix egg and ½ cup milk. Dip meat into egg-milk mixture, then into the 1 cup flour. Place oil in a 10-inch frying pan. Let oil get hot. Fry meat on medium heat, turning to brown 5 to 8 minutes on each side. Remove to serving platter. Pour all but 2 tablespoons oil from skillet. Stir 2 tablespoons flour into the oil, scraping brown bits from pan. Cook until light brown, about 3 minutes. Pour in the remaining 1 cup milk, stirring constantly. If gravy becomes thicker than you want, add more milk. Season with salt and pepper to taste. Serve gravy over meat or as a side dish with meat. *Yields 4 servings.*

GOOD AND EASY CHILI

1½ lb. ground chuck
1 cup chopped onions
½ cup chopped green pepper
1 tsp. salt
¼ tsp. black pepper
2 16-oz. cans tomatoes
2 16-oz. cans chili hot beans
1 tbsp. soy sauce

Cook ground chuck, onion, and green pepper in a dutch oven until brown, about 10 minutes, stirring to break up meat as it browns. Remove from heat and drain. Add salt and pepper. Set aside. Place tomatoes in blender until smooth. Add tomatoes, chili beans, and soy sauce to meat. This chili mixture can be placed in a crock-pot to cook for hours unattended. If cooked in dutch oven, place back on heat, bring to a boil, then cover pot and turn heat to simmer. Simmer at least 1 hour, stirring every 15 to 20 minutes. Serve hot with crackers or corn bread. *Yields 8 servings.*

HAM AND SPINACH PIE

1 10-oz. pkg. frozen chopped spinach,
   thawed and drained
½ cup grated parmesan cheese
⅓ cup butter
¼ cup finely chopped almonds
2 tbsp. finely chopped onion
¼ tsp. salt
2 cups chopped ham

Place spinach between double thickness of paper towels. Press out excess moisture. In mixer bowl, combine spinach, parmesan cheese, butter, almonds, onion, salt, and ham. Mix well. Set aside. Prepare crust.

CRUST

1½ cups all-purpose flour
½ tsp. salt
½ cup shortening
¾ cup cream-style cottage cheese, sieved

Mix together flour and salt. Cut in shortening with pastry blender. Add cottage cheese. Toss with fork until all is moistened. Form into a ball, then half it. Roll out half, and fit into a 9-inch pie pan. Spoon ham and spinach mixture into pie shell. Roll out remaining crust. Place over top of pie. Punch holes in top with a fork for steam to escape. Bake for 30 to 35 minutes in a 350-degree oven. *Yields 6 servings.*

HAM, POTATO, AND CHEESE CASSEROLE

2 cups diced potatoes
Water
1½ cups chopped cooked ham
¼ lb. cheddar cheese, chopped fine or grated
½ cup cream

Peel potatoes. Cut into cubes. Cover with water and boil for 10 minutes. Drain. Place in a 1½-quart casserole. Add ham, cheese, and cream. Bake in a 350-degree oven for 25 to 30 minutes, until bubbly. *Yields 4 to 6 servings.*

HAMBURGER BEANS

1 lb. ground hamburger meat
1 cup chopped onions
1 bell pepper, seeded and chopped
½ tsp. salt
¼ tsp. pepper
2 16-oz. cans pork and beans
½ cup ketchup
1 tbsp. brown sugar
1 tsp. mustard

In a heavy skillet, cook ground beef, onion, and pepper, stirring to break the meat apart as it cooks for 5 to 8 minutes. Remove from heat and drain. Mix in remaining ingredients. Return to heat and cook, stirring often for about 10 minutes, until hot and bubbling. *Yields 8 servings.*

HAMBURGER MACARONI AND CHEESE

1 box macaroni and cheese dinner
1 lb. hamburger meat
½ cup chopped onion
½ cup chopped celery
1 8-oz. can tomato paste
1 16½-oz. can whole-kernel corn, drained

Prepare macaroni and cheese as directed on package. Set aside. In skillet, cook hamburger meat, onion, and celery, stirring to break up meat as it cooks for 5 to 8 minutes. Remove from heat. Drain off fat. Mix together macaroni and cheese, hamburger, tomato paste, and corn. Pour mixture into a 2-quart casserole. Place in a 350-degree oven for 20 minutes, or until heated through. *Yields 6 to 8 servings.*

MACARONI AND CHEESE

1 8-oz. pkg. elbow macaroni
2 tbsp. butter or margarine
2 tbsp. flour
½ tsp. salt
⅛ tsp. pepper
1 cup milk
8 oz. Velveeta cheese, cut into chunks

Cook macaroni as directed on package. Place butter and flour in a heavy saucepan. Stir over medium heat until well combined, about 3 minutes. Add salt, pepper, and milk, stirring until smooth. Add cheese, stirring constantly for 5 to 8 minutes, or until cheese melts. Remove from heat. Stir in macaroni. Pour into serving bowl. *Yields 6 to 8 servings.*

MEXICAN LASAGNA

1 lb. ground beef
1 16-oz. can tomatoes, chopped
1 1⅛-oz. pkg. taco seasoning
1 2.8-oz. can french fried onions
1 12-oz. carton cottage cheese
1½ cups shredded cheddar cheese
2 eggs, beaten
12 6-inch flour tortillas

In skillet, brown ground beef for 5 to 8 minutes. Remove from heat. Drain. Add tomatoes and taco seasoning. Return to heat and simmer for 5 minutes. Stir in half of the fried onions. Remove from heat and set aside. In a mixing bowl, combine cottage cheese, 1 cup cheddar cheese, and eggs.

Place three tortillas on bottom of a greased 8-by-12-inch baking dish. Overlap six tortillas around sides. Spoon meat mixture over tortillas. Top with three remaining tortillas. Spoon cheese mixture over all. Cover dish with foil. Bake in a 350-degree oven for 45 minutes. Remove from oven. Sprinkle with remaining cheddar cheese and onions. *Yields 6 servings.*

PANHANDLER EGG PIE

½ lb. pork sausage
1 12-oz. pkg. frozen hash brown potatoes, thawed
8 large eggs
¼ cup half-and-half
Salt and pepper, to taste

In a skillet, brown sausage for 5 to 8 minutes, stirring to break apart as it browns. Remove from heat. Drain, reserving drippings. Set aside. In a clean skillet, cook potatoes in reserved drippings until soft, about 10 minutes. Spoon into a greased 10-inch pie pan. Shape potatoes into a pie shell. Set aside. Beat together eggs and half-and-half. Add sausage, salt, and pepper. Pour over potatoes. Bake in a 350-degree oven for 25 minutes, or until eggs are set. *Yields 8 servings.*

PARMESAN CHICKEN BAKE

½ cup dry bread crumbs
3 tbsp. grated parmesan cheese
1 tbsp. parsley flakes
1 tsp. salt
¼ tsp. lemon pepper
⅛ tsp. thyme
4 tbsp. melted margarine
3 chicken breasts, split and skinned

Combine bread crumbs, cheese, and seasonings in shallow dish. Set aside. Melt margarine in a baking dish. Dip chicken in margarine, then in crumbs to coat. Place chicken in melted margarine in baking dish. Bake in a 350-degree oven for 1 hour, basting with the margarine after 30 minutes. *Yields 6 servings.*

PIZZA CASSEROLE

1 lb. hot pork sausage
1 cup pizza sauce
2 cups shredded mozzarella cheese
1 cup self-rising flour
¾ cup milk
1 tbsp. cooking oil
2 eggs, beaten

Cook sausage for 5 to 8 minutes, or until brown, stirring to crumble as it cooks. Remove from heat and drain. Spread evenly in an 8-inch-square pan. Top with pizza sauce and cheese. Set aside. Mix together flour, milk, oil, and eggs until smooth. Pour over sausage mixture. Bake in a 400-degree oven for 30 to 35 minutes, or until top is brown. *Yields 6 servings.*

PORK CHOPS AND POTATO CASSEROLE

6 pork chops
¼ cup water
1 10-oz. can cream of mushroom soup
½ cup sour cream
4 medium potatoes, peeled and sliced thin
½ tsp. salt
¼ tsp. black pepper

In a heavy skillet over medium heat, brown pork chops for 5 to 8 minutes on each side. Remove chops from skillet and set aside. Drain fat from skillet. Pour water into skillet, scraping to remove brown bits. Mix in soup and sour cream. Place pork chops in a 2-quart casserole. Cover with potato slices. Add salt and pepper. Pour soup mixture over potatoes. Cover dish and bake in a 350-degree oven for 1 hour, or until potatoes are tender. Remove from oven. Let set for 10 minutes before serving. *Yields 6 servings.*

PORK SAUSAGE DRESSING

1 lb. hot pork sausage
1 cup onion, chopped
1 cup celery, chopped
5 cups corn bread crumbs
3 cups bread crumbs
2 tsp. sage
¼ tsp. black pepper
1 tsp. salt (or to taste)
3 to 3½ cups chicken broth
2 eggs, beaten

In a skillet, cook sausage, onion, and celery for 5 to 8 minutes, stirring to crumble sausage as it cooks. Remove from heat. Drain off fat. Mix with remaining ingredients. Place in a greased 13-by-9-inch baking pan. Bake in a 350-degree oven for 35 to 40 minutes. *Yields 12 servings.*

PRONTO PUPS

1 cup self-rising cornmeal
1 cup self-rising flour
⅔ cup buttermilk
2 eggs, beaten
1 lb. hot dogs
Mustard

Mix first four ingredients together. Insert wooden stick in end of hot dog. Dip in batter. Fry in deep hot oil until brown. Brush on mustard. *Makes enough batter for 1 pound of hot dogs.*

POTATO-HAM SCALLOP

2 cups cubed cooked ham
6 cups thinly sliced potatoes
   (6 to 8 medium)
¼ cup finely chopped onion
1 tsp. salt
½ tsp. pepper
⅓ cup flour
2 cups milk
½ cup corn flake crumbs
1 tbsp. butter, melted

Place half the ham in a 2-quart casserole. Cover with half the potatoes and half the onion. Sprinkle with ½ teaspoon salt and ¼ teaspoon pepper. Sift half of flour over all. Repeat layering ham, potatoes, and onion. Sprinkle with remaining salt and pepper. Sift remaining flour on top. Pour milk over all. Bake covered at 350 degrees until potatoes are tender, about 1 hour. Remove from oven and set aside.

Combine corn flake crumbs and melted butter. Remove cover and sprinkle on top of casserole. Return to oven and bake 15 minutes longer, until top is brown. *Yields 6 to 8 servings.*

RED BEANS AND RICE

2 16-oz. cans kidney beans
1 cup chopped onion
¼ tsp. garlic salt
1 lb. smoked sausage, sliced
1 10-oz. can tomatoes and green chilies
1 16-oz. can tomatoes, chopped
Cooked rice

Combine all ingredients in a large pot. Simmer for 1 hour. Serve over hot cooked rice. *Yields 6 to 8 servings.*

QUICK MACARONI AND CHEESE

1 cup butter-flavored cracker crumbs
2 cups cooked elbow macaroni
½ tsp. salt
½ cup butter or margarine
2 cups shredded cheddar cheese
1 cup milk

In a 2-quart buttered casserole dish, place ½ cup cracker crumbs. Spoon 1 cup macaroni over crumbs. Sprinkle with half the salt. Dot with half the butter. Sprinkle on half the cheese. With remaining ingredients, repeat layers of macaroni, salt, butter, and cheese. Spread remaining cracker crumbs on top. Pour milk over all. Bake in a 350-degree oven for 30 minutes. *Yields 6 to 8 servings.*

RICE KRISPIES CHICKEN

After you finish off the chicken, or even during the meal, make sure you scrape up the Rice Krispies crumbs in the bottom of the pan. It's mighty good eatin'!

1 frying-sized chicken, cut in serving pieces
3 tsp. salt
Water
5 cups crushed Rice Krispies cereal
½ cup margarine, melted

Place chicken in a large pan. Sprinkle with salt. Cover with water, stirring around to dissolve salt. Drain and set aside. Put Rice Krispies in a large bowl. Crush with hands. (You may need more than 5 cups.) Dip chicken in melted margarine, then in Rice Krispies. Place on shallow baking sheet. Drizzle any leftover margarine over chicken. Bake in a 350-degree oven for 1 hour, or until chicken is brown. *Yields about 8 servings.*

ROUND STEAK AND ONION GRAVY

1 round steak, about 2 lb.
Meat tenderizer
1½ cups water
2 tbsp. self-rising flour
½ tsp. salt (or to taste)
¼ tsp. black pepper
¼ tsp. Kitchen Bouquet
1 medium onion, sliced

Prick steak on both sides with fork. Sprinkle with meat tenderizer and rub in. Place in a lightly greased dutch oven over medium heat, then brown on each side for 5 to 8 minutes. Remove to platter and set aside.

Make a paste of 1 cup water and the 2 tablespoons flour. Pour into dutch oven where meat was cooked. Add remaining ½ cup water. Stir to scrape up any brown bits. Add salt, pepper, Kitchen Bouquet, and onion. Cook while stirring until thickened, about 3 minutes. Place steak back in pot with gravy. Turn heat down to simmer. Cook for 20 minutes, or until meat is tender, adding more water if needed. *Yields 6 to 8 servings.*

SAUERKRAUT AND WIENERS

1 lb. wieners
1 16-oz. can chopped kraut

Cut each wiener into four pieces. In saucepan, mix together the wieners and kraut. Cook covered for 15 to 20 minutes. *Yields 8 servings.*

SALISBURY STEAKS AND GRAVY

    1 lb. ground chuck
    1 egg, beaten
    ¼ cup soy sauce
    ½ tsp. salt
    ¼ tsp. pepper
    2 tsp. dried onion flakes
    ½ cup fine bread crumbs
    1 tbsp. oil

Mix together all ingredients except oil. Shape into 4 patties. Place oil in skillet. Add patties and brown on both sides, about 5 minutes for each side. Remove to a 2-quart casserole dish. Set aside. *Yields 4 servings.*

GRAVY

    2 tbsp. drippings (add more oil if not enough drippings)
    2 tbsp. flour
    1½ cups milk
    ½ tsp. salt
    ¼ tsp. pepper
    ½ tsp. Kitchen Bouquet

Mix drippings and flour in skillet. Cook until light brown, 2 to 3 minutes, scraping up brown bits as it cooks. Add milk, stirring constantly. Mix in salt, pepper, and Kitchen Bouquet. Cook until bubbly and thick, about 5 minutes. Pour over steaks. Cover and bake in a 350-degree oven for 20 minutes.

SAUSAGE AND EGG TORTILLAS WITH CHEESE SAUCE

8 flour tortillas
½ lb. pork sausage
4 eggs
2 tbsp. cream or evaporated milk
½ tsp. salt
⅛ tsp. black pepper
2 tbsp. butter or margarine
½ cup shredded cheddar cheese

Wrap tortillas in foil. Bake in a 350-degree oven for 15 minutes. Remove from oven. Set aside. Cook sausage in skillet until brown, 5 to 8 minutes, stirring to break apart as it cooks. Drain and set aside.

Beat eggs and add cream, salt, and pepper. Melt butter in clean skillet. Add eggs. Cook, stirring often until eggs are firm but still moist, about 5 minutes. Add sausage and cheese. Spoon equal amounts of sausage mixture into center of each warm tortilla. Roll up tortillas. Serve with cheese sauce. *Yields 8 servings.*

CHEESE SAUCE

2 tbsp. butter or margarine
2 tbsp. flour
½ tsp. salt
⅛ tsp. pepper
1 cup milk
8 oz. cubed Velveeta cheese

Melt butter in heavy saucepan over medium heat. Stir in flour and seasonings. Slowly add milk. Cook, stirring constantly until mixture comes to a boil and thickens, 3 to 5 minutes. Remove from heat. Add cheese, beating until cheese melts. Serve over sausage and egg tortillas.

SAUSAGE PIZZA

⅔ cup milk
2 cups biscuit baking mix
1 lb. hot pork sausage
1 8-oz. can tomato sauce
½ cup parmesan cheese
½ tsp. oregano leaves
2 cups grated mozzarella cheese

Mix together milk and baking mix. Knead on floured surface until smooth. Roll out dough to fit a lightly greased 10-inch pizza pan. Bake in a 375-degree oven for about 10 minutes, or until light brown. Remove from oven to cool while preparing other ingredients.

In a skillet, brown sausage for 5 to 8 minutes, breaking it up as it browns. Remove from heat and drain. Spread crust with tomato sauce. Sprinkle on parmesan cheese, oregano, sausage, and mozzarella. Return to oven for 5 to 10 minutes, or until cheese melts. *Yields 6 to 8 servings.*

SLOPPY JOES

2 lb. ground beef
1 cup chopped onion
½ tsp. salt
¼ tsp. black pepper
1 10-oz. can cream of tomato soup, undiluted
Hamburger buns

In a skillet, brown ground beef and onions for 8 to 10 minutes, stirring to break beef apart as it cooks. Drain. Place back in skillet. Add salt, pepper, and tomato soup. Stir to combine. Let simmer about 10 minutes. Serve over hamburger buns. *Yields about 8 servings.*

SHRIMP CREOLE

¼ cup butter or margarine
½ cup chopped onion
½ cup chopped green pepper
2 tbsp. self-rising flour
1 cup water
1 8-oz. can tomato sauce
½ tsp. salt
¼ tsp. black pepper
½ tsp. hot sauce
1 lb. shrimp, peeled and deveined
Cooked rice

Place butter in heavy skillet to melt. Add onion and pepper. Cook until slightly tender, about 5 minutes. Add flour and cook for 1 minute, stirring constantly. Stir in water, tomato sauce, salt, pepper, and hot sauce. Cover and simmer about 10 minutes. Add shrimp. Cook covered for 10 minutes longer. Serve over cooked rice. *Yields 6 servings.*

SPANISH RICE

¼ cup butter or margarine
1½ cups minute rice
1 medium onion, thinly sliced
½ cup chopped green pepper
1½ cups water
1 8-oz. can tomato sauce
1 tsp. salt
½ tsp. mustard

Melt butter in large skillet. Add rice, onion, and green pepper. Cook over medium heat while stirring for about 5 minutes, or until vegetables are tender. Add water, tomato sauce, salt, and mustard. Bring to a boil. Reduce heat and simmer with lid on for 5 minutes. Remove from heat. Let set about 5 minutes before serving. *Yields 6 to 8 servings.*

SOUR CREAM MEAT PIES

1½ cups ground beef
½ cup onion, chopped
½ cup mushrooms, chopped
1 cup sour cream (8-oz. carton)
½ tsp. salt
¼ tsp. pepper
2 cups self-rising flour
1 tbsp. sugar
½ cup shortening
1 egg, separated
1 tbsp. water

Brown ground beef and onion for about 5 minutes, breaking up as it browns. Drain fat. Add mushrooms. Remove from heat. Stir in ½ cup sour cream, salt, and pepper. Set aside.

Mix flour and sugar in bowl. Cut in shortening. Set aside. Mix egg yolk and remaining sour cream. Add to flour mixture and mix well. Roll out on floured surface. Cut into circles with sour cream carton. Place 1 heaping teaspoon of meat filling on one side of circle. Fold over. Seal edges with a fork. Mix egg white with water. Brush over pies. Bake in a 400-degree oven for 15 to 20 minutes, or until brown. *Yields 1½ dozen.*

TORTILLA CHICKEN

1 10-oz. bag tortilla chips
4 to 6 cups cooked chicken, chopped
1 10-oz. can tomatoes and green chilies, chopped
1 10¾-oz. can cream of mushroom soup
2 cups grated cheddar cheese

Line bottom of a 13-by-9-inch pan with half of tortilla chips. Place chicken over tortilla chips. Set aside.

Mix together tomatoes and soup. Spoon over chicken. Cover with remaining crushed tortilla chips and grated cheese. Bake in a 350-degree oven for 15 to 20 minutes, or until hot and bubbly. *Yields 12 servings.*

STUFFED PEPPERS

2 qt. water
4 bell peppers
½ lb. ground chuck
2 tsp. dried onion flakes
¼ cup evaporated milk
½ cup bread crumbs
¼ tsp. salt
⅛ tsp. pepper
1 8-oz. can tomato sauce

In a large saucepan, bring water to a boil. Cut tops from peppers and remove seeds. Drop peppers into boiling water and cook for 5 minutes. Remove from water. Drain and set aside.

Mix together ground chuck, onion flakes, milk, bread crumbs, salt, and pepper. Stuff peppers with meat mixture. Place in a deep baking dish. Pour tomato sauce over all. Bake in a 350-degree oven for 45 minutes. *Yields 4 servings.*

TACOS

1 lb. ground beef
¾ cup barbecue sauce
¼ cup water
½ cup chopped onion
1 tsp. chili powder
6 taco shells
1 cup chopped tomatoes
2 cups shredded lettuce
1 cup sharp cheddar cheese

Brown ground beef for 5 to 8 minutes, stirring to break it apart as it browns. Remove from heat. Drain. Add barbecue sauce, water, onion, and chili powder. Simmer 10 minutes, stirring occasionally. Fill taco shells with meat mixture. Top with tomatoes, lettuce, and cheese. *Yields 6 servings.*

VEAL CUTLETS PARMESAN

2 eggs
½ tsp. salt
¼ tsp. black pepper
1 cup bread crumbs
3 tbsp. grated parmesan cheese
1 lb. veal cutlets
6 tbsp. olive oil
1 8-oz. can seasoned tomato sauce
½ lb. grated mozzarella cheese

Beat eggs. Add salt and pepper. Set aside. Mix crumbs with parmesan cheese. Dip cutlets in egg mixture, then in bread crumbs. Fry cutlets in oil for 10 minutes, 5 minutes on each side, or until brown. Place in baking dish. Pour tomato sauce over cutlets. Sprinkle with mozzarella cheese. Bake in a 350-degree oven for 15 minutes, or until cheese is light brown. *Yields 4 to 6 servings.*

STORIES

PLEASE TAKE ME AWAY

Having stayed with my very sick aunt for three nights, and not gotten much sleep, I was exhausted; and I still had a two-hour drive ahead of me to get home. After driving for about an hour, I came upon a roadblock. The highway patrol was stopping everyone, checking drivers' licenses and registrations. My driver's license was in my billfold, but I couldn't find the registration. The patrolman told me to pull over and look in the glove compartment to see if I could find it.

The line of traffic was long. It seemed like everyone who passed stared at me, and I felt sure they were thinking I was a criminal who had gotten caught in the roadblock. I sat there in the heat for what seemed like an hour. It was one o'clock and I hadn't eaten lunch. It looked as though the patrolman had forgotten about me. I tooted my horn and finally got his attention, saying, "I can't find the registration. I'm so hot and tired and hungry, will you please either let me go or take me to jail where I can get some rest?"

He said, "Lady, are you alright?" I assured him I'd be okay. He felt sorry for me and let me go, but I honestly would have welcomed a nice cool jail cell with nothing to do but sleep, knowing what would be waiting for me when I got home: dirty dishes, dirty clothes, not to mention the condition of the rest of the house. But alas! No comfortable jail cell for me this time. I had to go home and take my punishment.

MY LITTLE CHURCH IN THE WILDWOOD

I was invited to the dedication of a new church in my home town. It was a beautiful new brick building, about one mile from the old church I attended when I was a child. After the preaching, dinner on the ground, and the hugs and handshakes were over, I felt drawn to the old church-site. To my horror, as we approached the beautifully shaded church yard where I had played as a child, I saw a barbed wire fence around it, and cows lying all around the old church house. The big double doors had been removed, and I could see hay and more cattle inside. It broke my heart to see the old church I loved so much being used for a barn.

I spent the rest of the afternoon with friends, and I was about to start my journey back to the big city where we lived when I felt I just had to visit the old church once more. It was getting dark, but by the time I reached the churchsite the moon was shining, and it was bright as day. There the old church stood in the moonlight, with cattle all around and hay filling the doorway. The brightest star I had ever seen shown directly over head, and a hazy halo seemed to arch across the top of the old church. I imagined I could almost see the baby Jesus lying in a cradle in the hay.

Jesus was still in the little church where I first found him and learned of his wonderful love so many years ago. The sadness lifted from my heart, and joyful memories of my childhood in my little church in the wildwood came flooding back.

BALD CAN BE BEAUTIFUL

Bald, men count your blessings; or as Elvis said, "Hair today, gone tomorrow." I saw a man on T.V. who had gone through torture to have a hair transplant. When he lifted the bloody bandage, his head looked like a bare yard that had been sodded. He had to go through this excruciating ordeal three times before the hair would begin to take root and grow. I say, "Why bother?"

Just think of all the advantages of being bald. If our teenage son had been bald, we'd have saved enough money on shampoo alone to put him through college. We would also have had clog-free drains, plenty of hot water, and dry towels. It would greatly reduce the chance of my having a heart attack. Did you ever ride in a car going sixty miles per hour with the driver combing his hair?

Think of the good things in life that can be enjoyed if you are bald. You will save time by not having to go to the barber shop to get a haircut that you didn't want to look like a haircut anyway. You can wear a dark suit without worrying about dandruff fallout, and nice breezy days won't bother you a bit. You can wear those cute, sporty little hats without worrying about your hair being mussed when you pull it off. If you think hair anywhere is better than none, I'm sure you can grow a nice beard. Bald men seem to have no trouble at all growing hair on their faces. Another consoling thought: look at Kojak, Trapper John, and Yul Brenner. They haven't done half bad.

NO LEFT TURN

A group of senior ladies asked me to take them to a nearby city for a meeting. This was a much larger city than I had ever driven in before, and I was a bit nervous. As we approached a busy intersection, I had my left blinker on. A policeman stood in the middle of the intersection waving his arms and shouting at me. I didn't know what he wanted me to do, so I just stopped! He yelled, "Lady, you can't turn left here!"

Thinking he must mean the street was too narrow for me to make the turn, I said, "I believe I could make it if you'd just move over a bit."

Exasperated, he said, "Lady, would you please just move on strait ahead!"

After we got through the intersection, one of the ladies said in a very quiet voice, "Dear, I think the sign said No Left Turn."

SAGGING MEMORIES

Before the automatic clothes dryer, a lot about a family's life was literally "hung out to dry." One could assume a lot about a family just by surveying the clothesline.

Diapers hanging on the line signified a child under two years old lived in the house. The colors and the type of clothes told you if it was a boy or girl; it used to be the color blue and pants for a boy, and pink and dresses for a girl. But it would be difficult to read a clothesline in the era in which we now live. Girls wear pants—even hi-top tennis shoes. Years ago, a pair of hi-top tennis shoes hanging by their tounges on a line definitely meant a boy lived at home. Many boys now wear what were formerly girls' colors. I haven't seen many boys wearing skirts or dresses; however, not many girls are wearing them either.

Clotheslines were a very important part of a young mother's and housewife's life in the "olden days" because that was the only means of drying the family laundry. I was very envious of anyone who had a nice taunt line with plenty of clothespins. My next door neighbor's clothesline posts were set in concrete. Four lines of rust-proof wire were stretched so taunt between the posts that they never sagged—no matter how many clothes were hung. Her clotheslines were in the side yard, so the lovely things hanging on them could be seen from the street.

The kind of clotheslines you had and what hung on them thus indicated how prosperous you were. My neighbor had beautiful clothes. I think she must have had new clothes she never actually washed; she just hung them on her lines for show. She was the first in the neighborhood with colored sheets and matching pillow cases. Those gorgeous blue and pink sheets hung on her lines two or three times a week, and they never looked faded. Another thing I envied about my neighbor: she was always home when her wash was on the line, and she could get it in if a sudden rain storm erupted. Oh! The agony of having sagging lines filled with dry clothes and it beginning to rain thirty minutes before you get off work.

Some of you younger people might ask, "What's she talking about? I never heard of a clothesline before?"

Well, honey, it's a line made of wire or rope stretched between two sagging posts, like I had; or two posts set in concrete, like my neighbor's; or between two trees, like Mama had. The trees held the lines taunt, but something was sure to come up with bird poop on it. It wasn't so bad if the birds hadn't had poke berries for lunch.

We've come a long way, ladies. To me, owning an automatic dryer beats the thrill of flaunting a new wardrobe on a clothesline anytime.

WHO'S CENSORING WHOM?

There was a time when we tried to be sure our children saw only movies with no foul language, nudity, or violence. But have times changed! Now we find our children telling us which movies are decent; and there are very few. When I told my daughter about a movie I planned to see, she said, "Mother, you shouldn't see that movie. It has a nude scene in it." I did the same thing she would have done had I told her she shouldn't see a particular movie: I saw it anyway. It could have been a good movie but for the nude scene, which was offensive to me.

Oh! But there was a movie coming out soon that I could see without being offended. It starred two of my favorite old-time stars. They surely felt the same way I did about nudity and obscene language in a film. I saw the female star of the picture on a talk show. She said that the reason she had not appeared in many movies in the last few years was because she refused to use foul language or play any bedroom scenes. I saw the movie, and bless her heart, she didn't say one bad word or go to bed with anyone; however, the rest of the cast sure did. The leading man, whom I had admired for years, needed his mouth washed out with soap. I was so disappointed and felt so embarrassed for him and his leading lady. The young boy, playing the role of their eleven-year-old grandson, had such filthy words to say. Some I had never heard before, and I thought I had heard them all. How could his parents allow their young son to say those words?

I guess I'm just old-fashioned, but this disappointment made me decide to save my movie money and save my memories of the old-time actors and actresses. I guess the money and the glory of being in just one more movie is more of a temptation than most can "bare."

BYE-BYE RADAR

I had just backed out of the driveway going shopping when I noticed Willie standing on the porch waving. He even ran out into the yard waving at me. I continued down the road thinking how sweet he was to run out and wave good-bye. About this time, our cat, Radar, peered down from over the top of the car. Another romantic moment spoiled! I got the cat down, turned around and carried her home. When I told Willie how good it made me feel when I thought he was waving good-bye, he said he'd do that more often. I said, "Never mind, it would never be the same. I'd always be expecting the cat to peer over the windshield."

TAKEN FOR GRANTED

Does your husband take you for granted? Maybe you should get your hair fixed.

As soon as Willie left for work, I put on my painting clothes, tied a kerchief around my uncombed hair, and went to work painting my white living room a lovely shade of green. I worked feverishly all day, and had just finished putting the furniture back in place when Willie drove into the driveway. I hurriedly pulled off the kerchief, ran my fingers through my hair, and met him at the door for my usual greeting, "Hi, what's for supper?" He settled himself in the easy chair and began reading the paper. I pulled the paper away and said, "Hey, don't you notice anything different?" He looked all around the room, then at me, grinned and said, "Oh yeah! You got your hair fixed. Looks good."

FISHING: THE FUN SPORT

Although I've lived with a fisherman for more than forty years, the magnetism of fishing is beyond me, and I guess will forever be. First of all, the weather never cooperates. It's either too hot or too cold; the wind is blowing too hard or from the wrong direction; or, of course, it's raining. However, none of the above will keep a true fisherman off the water. My home overlooks a lake, and many a rainy day I've witnessed the familiar picture of a couple of men donning yellow slickers bent over in eager anticipation of a stike. I've heard from my menfolk that fish bite better in the rain. I think maybe the fish simply think human beings are smart enough to come in out of the rain.

Of course, fish aren't the only animals out on the lake that bite.

Bugs, especially mosquitos and biting flies, provide plenty of activity when the fish aren't supportive. Ever dip a line during a swarm of Willow flies, or May flies as some call them? For those of us who have an aversion to bugs on our faces or in our hair; well, it's not a good place to be. Possibly you've heard the expression, "Don't rock the boat." Believe you me, I did exactly that, flailing my arms and shaking my head. Those kind of reactions don't endear one to a fisherman, I'm hear to tell ya.

Then there's the problem with live bait. I see all the beautiful, shiney, sparkling artificial lures in my sons' and husband's tackle boxes, and I wonder why it's ever necessary to mess with worms and minnows. But I'm told the real thing works best, even though plastic worms and minnow imitations abound. And those imitations cost a lot of money; there's more value in each of their tackle boxes than in my jewelry box. When I ask the reason for all the lures if they're not being used, I get the answer, "They're there just in case." Personally, I believe they're a kind of men's jewelry. They're all the time taking the lures out of the box to gaze at them in wonder, making them jiggle and wiggle and spin, then rearranging them for another day.

I think sometimes the fisherman forgets that when the catch is brought home, cleaning and cooking remains to be done. Often that problem is solved by handing the reigns to us land dwellers. No thanks! I can handle the cooking part, at least once every week or two, but I've long since canceled my participation in fish cleaning.

One more thing about fishing I don't understand: Why is it that the fish always bite better on the other side of the lake? I'll never figure out why my husband and sons go to the opposite end of the lake to try their luck, while the fishermen on the other side come almost to our front door. Why?

A THIRD LANGUAGE

I'm sure Juan, my son's college roommate from Columbia, South America, who was studying the English language at the University of Tennessee, thought he had encountered a completely new language to conquer when he met me. My southern accent and dialect were completely Greek to him—a part of the English language he had not yet experienced. When he came to our home, I greeted him, saying, "Juan, I'm so glad to see you! How you been makin' it?" He looked confused and replied in broken English, "What is this makin' it?" I said, "How y'all been doin'?" He tilted his head to one side with an even more confused look, so I tried again, saying, "How are you?" Juan's face lit up with a big grin and he said, "Fine, Fine! How . . . are . . . you?"

MACHINES TAKING OVER?

I'll believe it when I hear it. Our local grocery store just installed new cash registers that talk. As the cashier rings up the price of an item, a voice calls it out. I wonder what would happen if it called out the wrong price and you tried to argue with it. I just can't imagine machines taking over our society. If ever I walk into that friendly grocery store and a machine says, "Hi there, how are ya? If you need any help just holler," then I'll believe it.

MONEY TALKS

The local high school was offering classes to prepare for the G.E.D. test. Although in my forties, I wanted the satisfaction of having a high school diploma. After completing the courses and passing the tests, I was told to send two dollars for postage and handling to my home town high school, and I would receive my diploma, just as if I had graduated. While proudly showing the diploma to my sister, and teasing her a little at the same time, I said, "I only went to school two nights a week for three months, and for two dollars accomplished the same thing that took you four years." Johnnie's answer was, "Yeah, but I didn't have the two dollars!"

PUSH-BUTTON DEFEAT

The clock on my car is two hours fast and I don't know how to set it. It will never be correct unless someone else sets it for me or I move to another time zone.

The same thing is true with our V.C.R. The clock is never right. My knowledge of the V.C.R. is very limited; however, I can insert a tape, push the play button, rewind, and remove the tape.

While we were contemplating buying a new television, a young salesman had a remote in each hand showing us how he could even call up a picture of another station in the corner. I said, "Do you have any televisions with just an off and on switch and a channel selector." He replied, "No ma'am, that's a thing ot the past."

I've have discovered not only is it difficult for us old dogs to learn the new tricks of life, but we're constantly having trouble remembering the old ones.

HANDCRAFTS: JUST NOT MY BOTTLE OF TURPENTINE

I do so admire handcrafts and those people who do them so beautifully, but it just doesn't work out for me. I signed up for a decoupage class at a local craft shop. The cost was fifteen dollars for six lessons. I was so excited! Now I would be a craft person! At the first lesson, all students were given a list of supplies needed for our first project. The list was long, but Mrs. Baker, the teacher and owner of the shop, said she would be glad to help us select everything needed right from her shop.

I decided to do a card box. Mrs. Baker said this would make a good first project. For my card box, I needed two kinds of paint, two brushes, varnish, turpentine, sand paper, steel wool, a finishing spray, roller, and a baby bottle. That's right—a baby bottle. We were to pour turpentine into the bottle, cut a hole on top of the nipple, place the paint brush in the turpentine, and push the handle of the brush through the hole in the nipple. This holds the brush upright and prevents it from getting one-sided and stiff. It really works if your brush is no bigger than a baby bottle. All my purchases came to a rather tidy sum. Added to the fifteen dollars for the lessons, it was going to make for quite an expensive card box. But what the heck? I'd have enough supplies to do several more projects.

Mrs. Baker was with me all the way as I sanded and polished. The result was a beautiful card box anyone would be proud of; however,

Mrs. Baker thought it lacked something. Perhaps some gold braid around the edge would add just the right touch. She said, "And of course you want to sign all your work. For this you need a very small brush and some india ink. I have those in the shop." Another $8.29, but not to worry. I could use the brush and ink to sign all my future projects.

The box was indeed beautiful, the gold braid being just the finishing touch it needed. I put all my leftover supplies in a big box and headed home with my treasure.

My next project would be a gift for my good friend, Mickey. I would do her daughter's wedding picture and present it to her for a Christmas gift. I had planned to use the paint left from the card box, but when I went to Mrs. Baker for help in selecting a plaque on which to mount the picture, she said that color would never do. She suggested the best color would be two shades of green: a light green for the background and a darker green for edging. The plaque and paint came to about twelve dollars.

Back home, all alone, without Mrs. Baker's help, I began work on the project. After preparing the plaque and letting it dry, the next step was to glue on the picture. I did that and left it overnight to dry. While I slept something terrible happened to that picture. I must not have used the roller enough to press out all the air bubbles, for a big bubble had raised up right in the middle of the bride's face! Not knowing what to do, I called Mrs. Baker. She assured me this often happened and recommended I use a razorblade to split the bubble and glue it down. I did as she advised, but the poor little bride looked as though she had had a face lift with the skin lapped over her nose. And the more I worked the worse it looked. I gave it to Mickey anyway. We had a good laugh over it and Mickey said, "I know how hard you must have worked on this, and after all it's the thought that counts."

I would like to donate my box filled with supplies to someone who has signed up for Mrs. Baker's class; however, I doubt if any of it would meet with her approval. My supplies would never do for someone else's chosen project.

Vegetables

With Stories about Mama

Potatoes JoAnn and Green Beans Amandine.

HELPFUL HINTS

• Use beef- or chicken-flavored bouillon cubes or granules to season vegetables. It gives them great flavor, and one teaspoon granules is only eight calories and less than one gram of fat.

• While cooking fresh vegetables, add a small amount of shortening. It will keep them from boiling over.

• The secret to thick and creamy, fresh-fried corn is the way it is cut from the cob. Using a very sharp knife, just barely cut the top off the kernels, then scrape the remaining juice and pulp from the cob.

• Drop fresh vegetables in leftover pickle juice, such as onion quarters or small hole onions, onion slices, fresh cucumbers, carrots, cauliflower, and celery. It gives them a terrific taste.

BEANS, BEANS, BEANS

1½ lb. ground beef
1 pkg. dried onion soup mix
1 15-oz. can red kidney beans
1 15-oz. can pinto beans
1 15-oz. can Great Northern beans
½ cup chili sauce
1½ cups water
½ tsp. salt
¼ tsp. black pepper
½ tsp. chili powder

In a large, heavy saucepan, brown ground beef for 5 to 8 minutes, stirring to break apart as it cooks. Remove from heat and drain off fat. Place back on heat. Add soup mix, beans, chili sauce, water, and seasonings. Bring to a boil. Turn heat down to simmer. Let simmer, stirring occasionally for 30 minutes. Serve in bowls. *Yields 8 to 10 servings.*

CREAMED ONIONS AND CARROTS

½ cup diced celery
2 tbsp. butter or margarine
1 10-oz. can cream of chicken soup
½ cup sour cream
¼ cup dry white wine or water
2 tbsp. chopped parsley
1 lb. carrots, cooked and cut in half lengthwise
1 lb. small onions, cooked whole

In a heavy saucepan, cook celery in butter for about 5 minutes. Blend in soup and sour cream. Add wine and parsley. Stir in carrots and onions. Heat until bubbly, 5 to 8 minutes. *Yields 6 servings.*

COPPER PENNIES

1 lb. carrots
1½ cups boiling water
1 tsp. salt
1 tbsp. sugar
1 tsp. cornstarch
¼ tsp. ground ginger
¼ cup orange juice
Few drops yellow food coloring
2 tbsp. butter

Scrape and slice carrots fi inch thick. Place in saucepan with boiling water and salt. Cover pan and cook for 15 to 20 minutes, or until carrots are just tender. Drain and set aside. In a small saucepan, combine sugar, cornstarch, and ginger. Stir in orange juice and food coloring. Cook over low heat, stirring constantly until thickened, about 5 minutes. Remove from heat and stir in butter until melted. Pour over carrots. Toss to mix well. *Yields 6 to 8 servings.*

CROCK-POT POTATOES

About 6 medium potatoes
1 large onion
1 tsp. salt
¼ tsp. black pepper
1 11-oz. can cheddar cheese soup
¾ cup water

Peel potatoes and onion. Slice thin. Place in crock-pot, sprinkling with salt and pepper. Mix together cheese soup and water. Pour over potatoes. Cook on high for 3 to 5 hours, or until potatoes are tender. *Yields 6 to 8 servings.*

CRUSTY POTATO BALLS

4 medium-sized potatoes
Water
2 tbsp. milk
2 tbsp. butter
¼ tsp. salt
⅛ tsp. black pepper
½ cup grated parmesan cheese
2 tbsp. minced green onion
2 eggs, beaten
1 cup corn flake crumbs

Peel and dice potatoes. Put in saucepan. Cover with water and bring to a boil. Simmer 20 minutes and drain. Mash the potatoes and add milk, butter, salt, and pepper. Whip until smooth. Add cheese and onions. Chill at least 1 hour. Shape into small balls. Dip potato balls in beaten eggs, then roll in corn flake crumbs. Place on greased baking sheet. Bake in a 400-degree oven for 10 minutes, or until balls are hot and crusty. *Makes about 40 balls.*

EASY POTATOES AU GRATIN

6 medium-sized potatoes
1 tsp. salt
¼ tsp. black pepper
1 cup shredded cheddar cheese
1 cup milk

Cook potatoes with peel on until tender, about 20 minutes. Peel and grate. Place in a 2-quart casserole dish. Sprinkle with salt, pepper, and cheese. Pour milk over all. Bake in a 350-degree oven for 30 minutes, until brown. *Yields 6 to 8 servings.*

FANCY FRIED TATERS

6 slices bacon
4 cups chopped potatoes
1 cup chopped onion
1 tsp. salt
½ tsp. black pepper
¼ cup parmesan cheese

Cut bacon into small pieces. Fry in skillet on high heat until partly cooked, about 3 minutes. Add potatoes, onion, salt, and pepper. Turn heat to low. Put on tight-fitting lid. After about 10 minutes, turn to brown on other side. Cook about 5 minutes longer. Remove from heat. Lift out onto platter. Sprinkle with parmesan cheese. *Yields about 6 servings.*

FRIED ONION RINGS

2 large onions
Salt
1 cup evaporated milk
Self-rising flour
Oil

Cut onions in slices about ½ inch thick. Divide into rings. Sprinkle with salt and dip in milk, then in flour. Fry in hot oil until brown, about 3 minutes each side. *Yields 4 servings.*

FRIED SQUASH AND ONIONS

About 2 lb. yellow crook-neck squash
1 large onion, peeled and sliced
¼ cup margarine
1 tsp. salt
¼ tsp. pepper
½ cup flour

Wash and cut ends off squash. Slice. Peel onion and slice thin. Set aside. Place margarine in heavy skillet over low heat to melt. Cover bottom of skillet with half of squash. Sprinkle half of salt, pepper, and flour over squash. Spread half of onion over squash. Repeat with remaining ingredients. Cover skillet with tight-fitting lid. Cook for about 15 minutes. Turn with spatula and cook about 10 minutes longer to brown other side. *Yields 6 servings.*

GLAZED CARROTS

2 lb. carrots, scraped and sliced
1 cup water
¼ cup butter or margarine
¼ cup brown sugar
½ tsp. salt
1 tbsp. lemon juice

In a heavy saucepan, cook carrots in water for about 15 minutes, or until tender. Remove from heat. Place carrots in colander to drain. Set aside. Melt butter in saucepan and add sugar, salt, and lemon juice. Bring mixture to a boil, stirring constantly. Add carrots. Stir to coat. Remove from heat. Pour into serving bowl. *Yields 6 to 8 servings.*

GLAZED PEARL ONIONS AND CRANBERRIES

2 lb. small pearl onions, peeled
2 tbsp. butter
¼ cup sugar
2 cups cranberries
⅛ tsp. salt
⅓ cup water

In a heavy skillet, cook onions in butter, stirring to brown on all sides, 8 to 10 minutes. Add sugar, stirring to coat. Add cranberries and salt, stirring again to coat. Add water and stir, scraping up any brown bits from bottom of pan. Remove from heat. Pour into a 2-quart baking dish. Cover and bake in a 400-degree oven for about 30 minutes, until onion and cranberries are tender and glazed. *Yields 6 servings.*

GREEN BEAN CASSEROLE

1 16-oz. can French-style green beans
1 10-oz. can cream of mushroom soup
1 2.8-oz. can fried onion rings

Drain beans and place in casserole. Mix in soup and half of onions. Crumble and sprinkle remaining onions on top. Bake in a 350-degree oven for 30 minutes. *Yields 6 servings.*

GREEN BEANS AMANDINE

¼ cup butter or margarine
¼ cup slivered almonds
1 15-oz. can French-style green beans

Place butter in small skillet over low heat until melted. Add almonds and cook, stirring often until almonds are toasted, about 3 minutes. Heat green beans. Drain. Put in serving bowl. Pour almonds and butter over beans. Toss to mix. *Yields 4 servings.*

PICKLED CARROT STICKS

6 medium carrots
1 qt. water
2 tsp. salt
1 cup sugar
1 cup white vinegar
1 cup water
1 tbsp. mustard seed
1 stick cinnamon, broken into pieces
2 whole cloves

Scrape carrots and cut into 3-inch sticks. In a 2-quart saucepan, bring 1 quart water and salt to a boil. Drop in carrots and let cook for about 5 minutes. Drain and set aside. Mix sugar, vinegar, water, and mustard seeds together. Tie cinnamon and cloves in a cloth bag. Add to vinegar mixture. Let simmer for 10 minutes, stirring often. Pour over carrots. Cool. Place in a covered container. Refrigerate for several hours or overnight. Drain before serving. *Yields 10 to 12 servings.*

POTATOES JOANN

6 small potatoes
Water
4 slices bacon
Salt and pepper, to taste

Scrub potatoes, but do not peel. Place in large saucepan. Cover with water. Bring to a boil. Boil gently until potatoes are tender, about 20 minutes. Remove from heat and drain off water. Set aside. Cook bacon until crisp. Peel potatoes and cut into quarters. Place on platter. Sprinkle with salt and pepper and crumbled bacon. Pour hot bacon grease over potatoes. Serve hot. *Yields about 4 servings.*

RACY RICE AND CORN

1 cup uncooked regular rice
1 cup chopped onion
1 cup chopped green pepper
1 cup chopped celery
¼ cup butter or margarine
2 tsp. sugar
2 jalapeño peppers, seeded and finely chopped
1 cup shredded cheddar cheese
2 17-oz. cans cream-style corn

Cook rice according to package directions. Set aside. Sauté onion, green pepper, and celery in butter until tender, about 5 minutes. Remove from heat. Add rice, sugar, peppers, cheese, and corn, mixing well. Pour into a lightly greased 12-by-8-inch baking pan. Bake at 350 degrees for 45 minutes. *Yields 8 servings.*

SIMPLE STEAMED BROCCOLI

1 bunch broccoli
½ tsp. salt
1 cup shredded cheddar cheese

Cut off florets and peel stalks of broccoli. Place in steam basket over hot water. Steam for 15 to 20 minutes, until tender. Place on platter and sprinkle with salt and cheese. *Yields 6 servings.*

SKILLET BAKED BEANS

These beans are delicious, so why have a big electric or gas bill from baking beans?

2 16-oz. cans pork and beans
2 tbsp. brown sugar
2 tsp. dried onion flakes
1 tsp. mustard
½ cup ketchup
1 tbsp. fried meat grease

Mix all ingredients together in skillet. Simmer for about 15 minutes, stirring often. *Yields 6 servings.*

SPINACH CASSEROLE

1 15-oz. can spinach, drained
2 eggs, beaten
2 tsp. dried onion flakes
½ cup evaporated milk or cream
1 cup grated sharp cheddar cheese
4 pieces bacon, chopped and cooked crisp
12 round butter crackers, crushed
1 tbsp. butter or margarine

Mix first five ingredients in a 2-quart casserole. Sprinkle with bacon. Set aside. Mix cracker crumbs and margarine together. Sprinkle on top of casserole. Bake in a 350-degree oven for about 30 minutes, or until set and top is brown. *Yields 6 to 8 servings.*

SQUASH DRESSING

½ cup butter or margarine
1 cup chopped onion
1 cup chopped celery
2 cups cooked squash
2 cups corn bread crumbs
1 cup stale bread crumbs
2 10-oz. cans cream of chicken soup
2 eggs, beaten
2 tsp. sage
½ tsp. salt (or to taste)
¼ tsp. black pepper
⅛ tsp. cayenne pepper

Melt butter in skillet. Add onion and celery. Cook until tender, 5 to 8 minutes. In mixing bowl, mix onion, celery, and remaining ingredients. Spoon into a buttered casserole. Bake in a 350-degree oven for 40 to 45 minutes. *Yields 6 to 8 servings.*

STORIES

UNSELFISH LOVE

Mama was in her eighties and living alone during the hippy movement. Early one morning, she went out to the back yard and found a young man lying on the ground wrapped in a blanket. At first she thought he was dead. She stroked his cheek and called out, "Son!" He was sleeping or in a drugged daze, as he stirred to her touch.

She asked, "Who are you, son, and what are you doin' here?"

"I don't know, ma'am, but I'll leave."

"Don't you have some family or somebody I can call to come and get you?"

"No ma'am, don't call anyone. I'll just leave."

He was dirty and unshaven, and he looked around, seemingly oblivious to where he was. Mama said, "But son, you look cold and hungry. Come into the house and I'll fix you some breakfast while you take a bath and shave. I'll find you some of my son's clean clothes to put on."

He said, "No ma'am, I'll just go."

Mama watched him with sad and loving concern as he wondered off down the street. When she told us about the incident, of course we reprimanded her, reminding her of the dangers of befriending such a person; but, you see, at that time one of her grandsons was a wonderer. She didn't know where he was, and she explained, "I know it could've been dangerous. He could've even killed and robbed me; but all I could think of was that it could've been Bubba in a stranger's back yard, and I would hope that stranger would treat him kindly."

We hung our heads in shame, thinking had we been in Mama's shoes, how quickly our thoughts would have been only of our own welfare.

DEFINITELY A GENERATION GAP

When I was a child, the word pregnant was not normally used in the presence of children. The term was "in the family way," and it was kept secret as much as possible. Many children were told that the doctor brought their little brother or sister in his bag, or the stork brought the baby. Then there's the one about finding the baby under a cabbage leaf.

It was often said animals found their babies. While visiting my brother, Mama told our four-year-old daughter that Don's old hound dog had found nine puppies. "You mean she found them, Granny? She didn't have them?"

Mama said, "I don't understand this modern generation! It embarrasses me!"

HALF OFF: NOT ALWAYS A BARGAIN

I've heard it said that the only people you can depend on to tell the truth—no matter what the circumstance—are people over seventy and under seven. I've found this to be true, especially with my aging mother.

While shopping in a mall, we saw a sign in a boutique window: Clearance Sale. While we were browsing through several racks of very elaborate clothes, a sales girl approached us. She was wearing a black leather miniskirt, black leather vest, leather hi-heeled boots, an orange satin blouse, and a lot of dangly jewelry. She had on layers and layers of make-up, and her hair was about the color of her orange blouse and stood out in every direction. She said, "May I help you? Everything on this rack is half off."

Mama gave her a very critical up-and-down look and said, "Honey, anyone who'd buy anything in this store would have to be half off."

Cakes and Pies

With Stories about Sick Humor

Chocolate Ice Cream Cake.

HELPFUL HINTS

• Don't throw away the butter and margarine wrappers. There is usually enough butter or margarine left on the wrapper to grease cake and cookie pans.

• Cornstarch is good to use as a thickening agent for vanilla pudding and pies, but if you want your chocolate pies to be dark and rich looking, use flour instead. Cornstarch fades the chocolate and gives it a washed-out color.

CAKES

AMBROSIA CAKE

1½ cups butter, at room temperature
1 8-oz. pkg. cream cheese
3 cups sugar
5 eggs
2 eggs, separated
3 cups sifted all-purpose flour
2 tsp. baking powder
½ tsp. salt
1 tsp. orange extract
1 tsp. pineapple extract

In a large mixing bowl, cream together butter and cream cheese. Gradually add sugar. Add the 5 eggs plus yolks of the 2 eggs, beating thoroughly until smooth, and set aside. Reserve the 2 egg whites for icing. Sift together flour, baking powder, and salt. Fold into batter. Add extracts. Divide evenly among four greased and floured 9-inch cake pans. Bake in a 325-degree oven for 35 to 40 minutes, or until pick inserted in center comes out clean. Remove from oven. Cool in pans for 10 minutes. Turn out onto wire racks to cool.

FILLING

½ cup sugar
2 tbsp. cornstarch
1 cup orange juice
1 11-oz. can mandarin oranges, drained and cut into small pieces
1 20-oz. can crushed pineapple, drained
1 cup chopped pecans
2 3½-oz. cans flaked coconut

Combine sugar and cornstarch in a heavy saucepan. Gradually stir in orange juice. Cook over medium heat until thickened, about 5 minutes. Chill for about 1 hour. Fold in oranges, pineapple, pecans, and 1 can coconut. Place 1 cake layer on cake plate. Spread ⅓ of filling on cake. Repeat with remaining layers, leaving top plain. Cover sides and top with icing. Press remaining coconut on sides and on top of cake.

ICING

2 egg whites
½ cup light corn syrup
½ cup sugar
⅛ tsp. salt
1 tsp. vanilla

Combine egg whites, syrup, sugar, and salt in upper part of a double boiler. Beat with mixer until partly mixed. Set over boiling water. Cook for about 5 minutes, beating constantly until icing stands in peaks. Remove from hot water. Beat in vanilla. Spread on cake. *Yields 10 to 12 servings.*

ANGEL FOOD CAKE

12 egg whites
1 tsp. cream of tartar
⅛ tsp. salt
1½ cups sugar
1 cup sifted cake flour
1 tsp. vanilla

Beat egg whites until foamy. Add cream of tartar and salt. Continue beating until soft peaks form. Add sugar a little at a time, beating each time to mix sugar in well. Beat until very stiff. Sprinkle flour over egg whites ¼ cup at a time. Fold in gently. Fold in vanilla. Spoon batter into ungreased 10-inch tube pan, spreading evenly. Bake in a 325-degree oven for 45 minutes, or until cake springs back when touched. Remove from oven and invert pan. Cool in pan for about 45 minutes. Run knife around sides of pan to remove. *Yields 10 to 12 servings.*

APPLE DAPPLE CAKE

2 cups sugar
1 cup oil
3 eggs
3 cups self-rising flour
1 tsp. cinnamon
2 tsp. vanilla
3 cups peeled chopped apples
2 cups flaked coconut
1 cup chopped dates
1 cup chopped pecans

Mix sugar and oil together. Add eggs and beat well. Stir in flour, cinnamon, and vanilla. Add apples, coconut, dates, and pecans. Spoon batter into a greased and floured 10-inch tube pan. Bake in a 325-degree oven for 1½ hours, or until toothpick inserted in center comes out clean. Remove from oven. Leave cake in pan and spoon hot caramel topping over hot cake. Let cool in pan before removing cake.

CARAMEL TOPPING

1 cup brown sugar
½ cup milk
½ cup butter or margarine

Combine all ingredients in saucepan. Heat and stir until blended. Boil for 2 minutes. Spoon on cake while hot. *Yields 10 to 12 servings.*

APPLESAUCE CAKE

½ cup butter or margarine
2 cups sugar
2 eggs
2½ cups self-rising flour
½ tsp. baking soda
½ tsp. cinnamon
¼ tsp. nutmeg
¼ tsp. allspice
1½ cups applesauce
½ cup golden raisins
1 cup chopped nuts
½ tsp. vanilla

Cream together butter and sugar. Beat in eggs one at a time. Set aside. Sift together flour, baking soda, and spices. Add flour mixture to creamed mixture alternately with applesauce, beginning and ending with flour. Stir in raisins, nuts, and vanilla. Pour batter into a greased and floured 13-by-9-inch baking pan. Bake in a 350-degree oven for 45 minutes, or until pick inserted in center comes out clean. Frost as desired, or eat plain or with whipped cream. *Yields 12 servings.*

BUTTER CREAM ICING

1 cup shortening
¼ tsp. salt
½ tsp. vanilla
1 1-lb. box confectioners' sugar
⅓ cup milk

Beat together shortening, salt, and vanilla until creamy. Add sifted sugar alternately with milk, beating until creamy. *Makes enough to ice a three-layer cake.*

BANANA NUT CAKE

½ cup shortening
1½ cups sugar
3 eggs
½ tsp. baking soda
½ cup buttermilk
1 cup mashed bananas
1 tsp. vanilla
1 tsp. salt
2 tsp. baking powder
2 cups sifted flour
½ cup chopped pecans in 2 tbsp. flour

Cream together shortening and sugar. Add eggs one at a time, beating well after each addition. Set aside. Dissolve soda in buttermilk. Add buttermilk, banana, and vanilla to sugar mixture. Set aside. Sift together remaining dry ingredients. Add to banana mix. Beat until well blended. Fold in floured pecans. Divide batter into two greased and floured 9-inch cake pans. Bake in a 350-degree oven for 25 to 30 minutes, or until pick inserted in center comes out clean. Remove from oven and cool in pans for 10 minutes, then remove to wire racks.

ICING

2 tbsp. butter
½ cup mashed banana
3¼ cups sifted confectioners' sugar
1 tsp. vanilla
½ cup chopped pecans

Combine first four ingredients. Mix well. If too thick, thin with cream. Add pecans. Spread on cake. *Yields 10 to 12 servings.*

BANANA SPLIT CAKE

1½ cups graham cracker crumbs
½ cup margarine, softened
¼ cup sugar
1 8-oz. pkg. cream cheese,
 at room temperature
½ cup margarine, softened
2 cups sifted confectioners' sugar
2 eggs, beaten
4 large bananas, sliced lengthwise
1 20-oz. can crushed pineapple, drained
1 8-oz. carton whipped topping
1 cup chopped nuts
½ cup maraschino cherries,
 chopped and drained

Mix together cracker crumbs, margarine, and sugar. Press in bottom of a 13-by-9-inch pan. Set aside. Beat together cream cheese and margarine. Add confectioners' sugar and eggs. Beat until smooth. Spread over crumb mixture. Place sliced bananas over cream cheese layer. Place pineapple over bananas. Spread whipped topping over pineapple. Sprinkle with nuts and cherries. Chill in refrigerator for about 2 hours before serving. *Yields 12 servings.*

BUTTERNUT CAKE

1 cup shortening
2 cups sugar
4 eggs
2 cups self-rising flour
1 cup milk
1 tbsp. butternut flavoring

Cream together shortening and sugar. Add eggs, beating well. Add flour, mixing alternately with milk. Add flavoring. Pour into two greased and floured 9-inch cake pans. Bake in a 350-degree oven for 25 to 30 minutes, or until pick inserted in center comes out clean. Remove to racks to cool.

ICING

½ cup margarine
1 8-oz. pkg. cream cheese
1 1-lb. box sifted confectioners' sugar
1 tbsp. butternut flavoring
1 cup chopped pecans

Cream together margarine and cream cheese. Beat in sugar and flavoring. Add pecans. Spread between layers and on top of cooled cake. *Yields 10 to 12 servings.*

CARROT-PINEAPPLE-COCONUT CAKE

2 cups self-rising flour
½ tsp. baking soda
1 tsp. cinnamon
3 eggs
2 cups sugar
1 cup cooking oil
1 8-oz. can crushed pineapple, undrained
2 cups grated carrots
1 cup coconut
1 cup chopped nuts
½ tsp. vanilla

Combine flour, soda, and cinnamon. Set aside. Beat eggs. Add sugar and oil, then add to flour mixture. Beat until smooth. Stir in pineapple, carrots, coconut, nuts, and vanilla. Pour into a greased and floured 13-by-9-inch pan. Bake in a 350-degree oven for 50 to 55 minutes, or until pick inserted in center comes out clean. Remove from oven. Prick holes in warm cake. Spoon on glaze.

LEMON GLAZE

⅓ cup sugar
2 tsp. water
2 tbsp. lemon juice

Mix together all ingredients in a heavy saucepan. Bring to a boil, and boil for 1 minute. Remove from heat and spoon on cake while hot. *Yields 12 servings.*

CHOCOLATE ICE CREAM CAKE

2 eggs, separated
½ cup sugar
1¼ cups all-purpose flour
1 cup sugar
½ cup cocoa
½ tsp. baking soda
¼ tsp. salt
½ cup oil
1 cup buttermilk
½ gallon ice cream
1 cup whipped cream

Beat egg whites and add ½ cup sugar. Beat until stiff. Set aside. Sift together flour, 1 cup sugar, cocoa, soda, and salt. Add oil, buttermilk, and egg yolks. Beat until smooth. Gently fold in egg whites. The layers should be thin, so use about 1⅔ cups batter in each of three greased and floured 9-inch cake pans. Bake at 350 degrees for 18 to 20 minutes, or until pick inserted in center comes out clean. Cool in pans for 5 minutes, then invert onto wire racks to cool. When cooled, wrap each layer and freeze.

Prepare ice cream layers. Line two of same pans used for cake with foil. Working quickly, spread slightly softened ice cream about ¾ inch deep in each pan. Cover tightly and freeze. Remove cake and ice cream from freezer. On serving plate, alternate layers of cake and ice cream, removing foil and beginning and ending with a cake layer. Frost top with whipped cream. Put back in freezer until serving time. Keep any leftover cake in freezer. *Yields 10 to 12 servings.*

CHOCOLATE SYRUP CAKE

½ cup butter or margarine
1 cup sugar
4 eggs
1 16-oz. can chocolate syrup
1 cup self-rising flour
½ tsp. vanilla

Cream together butter and sugar. Add eggs one at a time, beating after each addition. Add syrup. Mix well. Add flour and vanilla. Beat until smooth. Pour into a greased and floured 13-by-9-inch pan. Bake in a 350-degree oven for 30 minutes, or until pick inserted in center comes out clean. Remove from oven to cool.

ICING

2 cups sugar
⅓ cup cocoa
½ cup milk
½ cup butter or margarine
½ tsp. vanilla

In a heavy saucepan, mix together sugar and cocoa. Stir in milk. Place over medium heat and bring to a boil. Boil for 2 minutes. Remove from heat. Add butter and vanilla. Beat until butter melts and mixture is smooth. Spread on cake. *Yields 12 servings.*

CHOCOLATE UPSIDE-DOWN CAKE

4 tbsp. butter
¼ cup brown sugar
⅔ cup light corn syrup
¼ cup heavy cream
1 cup chopped nuts

Melt butter in a heavy saucepan. Stir in brown sugar. Heat until bubbly, about 5 minutes. Stir in corn syrup and cream. Heat, stirring constantly until it comes to a boil, about 3 minutes. Remove from heat. Add nuts. Pour into greased and floured bundt pan. Let stand while preparing cake batter.

CAKE

1¾ cups flour
2 tsp. baking powder
¼ tsp. salt
6 tbsp. butter
1½ cups sugar
2 eggs, separated
3 squares unsweetened chocolate, melted
1 tsp. vanilla
1 cup milk

Sift together flour, baking powder, and salt. Set aside. Cream butter and sugar. Beat in egg yolks, melted chocolate, and vanilla. Add flour mixture alternately with milk. Beat egg whites until stiff. Fold into cake batter. Spoon batter over nut mixture in bundt pan. Bake at 350 degrees for 45 minutes, or until pick inserted in center comes out clean. Remove from oven. Let cool in pan for 10 minutes. Loosen cake from edge of pan. Cover with plate, invert, shake gently, then lift off pan. Spoon any nuts and syrup left in pan onto cake. *Yields 10 servings.*

COCONUT SOUR CREAM CAKE

1 box butter cake mix
2 cups sugar
1 8-oz. carton sour cream
1 12-oz. pkg. coconut
1 8-oz. container whipped topping

Prepare cake mix and bake according to package directions, using two 9-inch cake pans. Remove from oven and cool on wire racks. Combine sugar, sour cream, and all but ½ cup coconut. Set aside. Slice cake layers in half. Stack cake, and using all but 1 cup of mixture, spread sour cream mixture between layers. Mix whipped topping with reserved cup of sour cream mixture. Frost top and sides with whipped topping-sour cream mix. Sprinkle with the remaining ½ cup coconut. Keep refrigerated. Better if made a day or two before serving. *Yields 10 to 12 servings.*

CREAM CHEESE COFFEE CAKE

½ cup sugar
1 tsp. cinnamon
2 10-oz. cans butterflake biscuits
1 3-oz. pkg. cream cheese, cut into 20 pieces
1 cup chopped pecans
¼ cup butter or margarine, melted
1 cup sifted confectioners' sugar
2 tbsp. hot water
½ tsp. vanilla

Mix together sugar and cinnamon. Set aside. On a floured surface, roll biscuits into about a 3-inch circle. Place a piece of cream cheese in center of each circle. Sprinkle with small amount of sugar-cinnamon mixture and pecans. Pull sides up and pinch together to enclose the cream cheese, sugar-cinnamon, and pecans like a ball. Repeat procedure with all biscuits.

Place melted butter in a 10-inch tube pan. Sprinkle any leftover sugar-cinnamon and pecans over butter. Layer biscuit balls in pan seam-side up. Bake in a 350-degree oven for 30 to 35 minutes, or until brown. Remove from oven. Invert on serving plate. Combine confectioners' sugar, water, and vanilla. Drizzle over cake. *Yields 10 to 12 servings.*

CREAM CHEESE POUND CAKE

1 cup margarine, softened
½ cup butter, softened
1 8-oz. pkg. cream cheese, softened
3 cups sugar
6 eggs
3 cups sifted cake flour
1 tsp. vanilla

In a large mixing bowl, beat together margarine, butter, and cream cheese until smooth and creamy. Gradually add sugar, beating until fluffy. Add eggs one at a time, beating well after each addition. Stir in flour and vanilla. Spoon batter into a well-greased and floured 10-inch tube pan. Bake in a 325-degree oven for 1 hour 30 minutes, or until wooden pick inserted in center comes out clean. Remove from oven. Cool in pan for 10 minutes. Turn out on plate to cool. *Yields 10 to 12 servings.*

DIRT CAKE

This concoction may be prepared in a 13-by-9-inch dish. However, it will be a big hit if prepared in a flower pot and served up with a trowel.

> 1¼ lb. Oreo cookies
> ½ cup butter or margarine, softened
> 1 8-oz. pkg. cream cheese, softened
> 1 cup confectioners' sugar
> 1 12-oz. container whipped topping
> 1 6-oz. pkg. vanilla instant pudding mix

Crush cookies in a blender. Sprinkle half of crumbs evenly over bottom of flower pot or dish. Beat together butter and cream cheese. Add sugar and beat until creamy. Fold in whipped topping. Spread half of mixture over crumbs. Prepare pudding as directed. When thickened, spoon half over topping. Repeat layers, saving crumbs for top. Decorate with candy worms or flowers. Keep refrigerated. *Yields 12 or more servings.*

EASY CARROT CAKE

Using baby food carrots in this recipe eliminates the drudgery of grating fresh carrots.

2 cups all-purpose flour
2 tsp. baking soda
1 tsp. salt
1 tsp. cinnamon
2 cups sugar
1 cup oil
4 eggs
2 7-oz. jars carrots junior baby food
½ tsp. vanilla

Sift together flour, baking soda, salt, and cinnamon. Set aside. Mix together sugar and oil. Add eggs, beating to blend well. Mix in flour mixture, baby food, and vanilla. Pour into a greased and floured 13-by-9-inch baking pan. Bake in a 350-degree oven for 25 to 30 minutes, or until wooden pick inserted in center comes out clean. Remove from oven. Cool completely before icing.

ICING

1 3-oz. pkg. cream cheese, softened
¼ cup margarine, softened
2 cups sifted confectioners' sugar
½ cup chopped nuts
½ tsp. vanilla

Cream together cream cheese, margarine, and sugar. Stir in nuts and vanilla. Spread on cool cake. *Yields 12 servings.*

FRUIT COCKTAIL CAKE

2 eggs
1½ cups sugar
2 cups self-rising flour
¼ tsp. baking soda
1 15-oz. can fruit cocktail
½ cup brown sugar
½ cup chopped nuts

Beat eggs and add sugar. Set aside. Mix flour and soda together. Add to sugar-egg mixture. Stir in fruit cocktail. Pour into a greased 13-by-9-inch baking pan. Sprinkle brown sugar and nuts over top. Bake in a 350-degree oven for 45 minutes. Ice while hot.

ICING

½ cup sugar
½ cup evaporated milk
½ cup butter or margarine
½ tsp. vanilla
1 cup coconut

In a heavy saucepan, mix together sugar, milk, and butter. Bring to a full boil, stirring to mix in butter as it melts. Boil for 2 minutes, then remove from heat. Add vanilla and coconut. Spoon on cake while both cake and topping are hot. *Yields 12 servings.*

GERMAN CHOCOLATE CAKE

1 4-oz. pkg. German sweet chocolate
½ cup boiling water
1 cup butter or margarine
2 cups sugar
4 egg yolks, beaten
1 tsp. vanilla
2¼ cups all-purpose flour
1 tsp. baking soda
½ tsp. salt
1 cup buttermilk
4 egg whites, stiffly beaten

Melt chocolate in boiling water. Set aside to cool. Cream together butter and sugar. Add egg yolks, beating well. Beat in vanilla and chocolate. Set aside. Sift together flour, soda, and salt. Add alternately with buttermilk to chocolate mixture, beginning and ending with flour. Fold in stiffly beaten egg whites. Divide evenly into three greased and floured 9-inch cake pans. Bake in a 350-degree oven for 30 to 35 minutes, or until pick inserted in center comes out clean. Remove from pans to wire racks to cool.

COCONUT-PECAN ICING

1 cup evaporated milk
1 cup sugar
3 egg yolks, beaten
½ cup butter or margarine
1 tsp. vanilla
1 cup coconut
1 cup chopped pecans

In a heavy saucepan, combine milk, sugar, egg yolks, and butter. Cook and stir over medium heat for about 12 minutes, until thickened. Remove from heat. Add vanilla, coconut, and pecans. Cool until thick enough to spread. Spread between layers and on top of cake. *Yields 10 to 12 servings.*

LEMON-DROP CAKE

5 large eggs, separated
⅓ cup sugar
¼ tsp. salt
⅓ cup all-purpose flour
1½ cups hard lemon-drop candies, crushed fine
¼ cup confectioners' sugar
1 pint whipping cream

Beat egg yolks and 3 tablespoons of sugar until thick and pale. Set aside. With clean beaters, beat egg whites and salt until stiff. Gradually add remaining sugar, and beat until very stiff. Fold egg whites into yolk mixture alternately with flour until blended. Fold in ¼ cup crushed lemon-drops.

Line a 15½-by-10½-inch jelly-roll pan with wax paper. Grease and flour paper. Spread batter evenly into prepared pan. Bake in a 350-degree oven for 10 to 12 minutes, until top is brown and pick inserted in center comes out clean. Dust a clean kitchen towel with confectioners' sugar. Remove cake from oven and invert onto towel. Peel off wax paper and trim off crisp edges. Starting from narrow end, roll up cake and towel. Cool completely on rack.

Beat whipping cream until stiff. Fold in 1 cup crushed candy. Save ¼ cup for top. Unroll cooled cake. Remove towel. Spread half of cream mixture on cake and roll cake without towel. Place seam-side down on serving plate. Spread with remaining whipped cream. Sprinkle with remaining ¼ cup crushed lemon-drops. Refrigerate until served. *Yields 10 servings.*

NO-BAKE FRUITCAKE

1 cup evaporated milk
2 cups miniature marshmallows
1½ cups light golden raisins
¼ lb. red candied cherries
¼ lb. green candied cherries
¼ lb. red candied pineapple, chopped
¼ lb. green candied pineapple, chopped
½ lb. mixed candied fruit
1 cup coconut
3 cups nuts
3 cups graham cracker crumbs

Place milk and marshmallows in a heavy saucepan. Cook over low heat, stirring constantly to keep from sticking, until marshmallows are melted, 8 to 10 minutes. Set aside. In a large mixing bowl, mix raisins, candied fruits, coconut, nuts, and graham cracker crumbs. Pour milk and marshmallow mixture over all. Mix well.

Grease two 9-by-5-inch loaf pans with butter, and line with wax paper. Grease paper. Pack mixture in pans. Place in the refrigerator to cool completely. To serve, remove cakes from pans, peel off wax paper, and cut into slices. This cake will keep in refrigerator or freezer indefinitely. *Yields two 9-by-5-inch loaves.*

ORANGE CAKE

This cake is moist with a tangy taste, and oh so good!

1 pkg. white cake mix
1 3½-oz. pkg. lemon gelatin
¾ cup water
¾ cup oil
4 eggs

Mix all ingredients together in order given. Beat until smooth, about 3 minutes. Pour into a greased and floured 13-by-9-inch baking pan. Bake in a 325-degree oven for 35 to 40 minutes. Remove from oven. Cool for 10 minutes. Punch holes in cake with fork. Spoon on glaze. *Yields 12 servings.*

GLAZE

3 cups sifted confectioners' sugar
½ cup orange juice
¼ cup lemon juice

Mix all ingredients together. Spoon over hot cake.

ORANGE SLICE CAKE

This cake is much like a fruitcake.

1 cup butter
2 cups sugar
4 eggs
1 lb. dates, chopped
1 lb. orange slice candy, cut up
2 cups chopped nuts
1 cup shredded coconut
3½ cups all-purpose flour
1½ cups buttermilk
1 tsp. baking soda
½ tsp. salt

Cream butter and sugar together. Add eggs one at a time, beating well after each addition. Set aside. Mix dates, candy, nuts, and coconut with ½ cup flour. Set aside. Add ½ cup buttermilk to sugar mixture. Beat well. Set aside. Sift together remaining 3 cups flour, soda, and salt. Add to sugar mixture alternately with remaining buttermilk. Fold in date mixture. Spoon into a greased and floured 10-inch tube pan. Bake in a 250-degree oven for 2 hours 30 minutes, until pick inserted in center comes out clean. Remove from oven.

ICING

1 cup orange juice
2 cups sifted confectioners' sugar
2 tbsp. butter

Mix orange juice, confectioners' sugar, and butter in a saucepan. Heat, stirring until sugar and butter are melted, about 5 minutes. Spoon over hot cake in pan. Cool cake before removing from pan. *Yields 10 to 12 servings.*

PEAR CAKE

3 eggs, beaten
1¾ cups sugar
1 cup vegetable oil
1 tsp. vanilla
2½ cups all-purpose flour
2 tsp. baking powder
1 tsp. baking soda
½ tsp. salt
1 tsp. allspice
3 cups peeled and finely chopped pears
1 cup chopped pecans

In a large mixing bowl, beat eggs, sugar, and oil. Add vanilla. Set aside. Sift together flour, baking powder, soda, salt, and allspice. Mix flour mixture into oil-egg mixture a little at a time. Stir in pears and nuts. Batter will be stiff. Spoon into a well-greased and floured bundt pan. Bake in a 350-degree oven for 1 hour, or until wooden pick inserted in center comes out clean. Remove from oven. Cool in pan at least 10 minutes. Remove to cake plate. Top with icing. *Yields 10 to 12 servings.*

CARAMEL ICING

¼ cup butter or margarine
¼ cup packed brown sugar
2 tbsp. milk
1 cup sifted confectioners' sugar
¼ tsp. vanilla

Melt butter in a heavy saucepan. Add brown sugar. Cook and stir until smooth, about 3 minutes. Remove from heat. Add milk, confectioners' sugar, and vanilla. Beat until creamy smooth. Drizzle over cake.

PIÑA COLADA CAKE

My son Tim, who was just learning to cook, asked me for a cake recipe that would surprise and impress the ladies in the office where he worked. He made this cake all by himself, and it still turned out great. It was a big hit at coffee break.

> **1 pkg. yellow cake mix**
> **1 14-oz. can sweetened condensed milk**
> **1 8-oz. can cream of coconut**
> **1 12-oz. can crushed pineapple, drained**
> **1½ cups coconut**
> **1 12-oz. container whipped topping**
> **1 cup chopped nuts**

Prepare cake mix according to directions on box, baking in a 13-by-9-inch pan. Remove from oven and set aside. While cake is still hot, punch holes in it with a fork. Mix together condensed milk and cream of coconut. Spoon over cake. Let stand for about 1 hour. Mix together drained pineapple and 1 cup of coconut. Spread on cake. Cool completely. Cover with whipped topping. Sprinkle with remaining ½ cup coconut and chopped nuts. *Yields 12 servings.*

PINEAPPLE UPSIDE-DOWN CAKE

1 20-oz. can sliced pineapple
¼ cup butter or margarine
½ cup light brown sugar
Maraschino cherries
⅓ cup shortening
⅔ cup sugar
1 egg
1⅓ cups self-rising flour
¾ cup milk, plus 2 tbsp. pineapple juice

Drain pineapple, reserving 2 tablespoons juice. In a 10-inch iron skillet, melt butter. Add brown sugar, stirring around until sugar and butter are well blended. Remove from heat. Arrange pineapple slices over butter and brown sugar. Place a cherry in center of each slice. Set aside. Cream together shortening and sugar. Beat in egg. Add flour and milk alternately, beginning and ending with flour. Stir in 2 tablespoons pineapple juice. Spoon cake batter over pineapple slices in skillet. Bake in a 325-degree oven for 40 to 45 minutes, or until cake springs back when gently pressed with fingers. Remove from oven and let stand in skillet for 5 minutes. Turn out on serving plate. Spoon any sugar mixture left in skillet over top of cake. *Yields 6 to 8 servings.*

POUND CAKE

This is a very good plain pound cake. It's great as is, or topped with fruit and whipped cream as a shortcake.

    1½ cups sugar
    ½ cup butter, softened (do not substitute margarine)
    ¼ cup butter-flavored shortening
    3 eggs
    ½ tsp. vanilla
    1½ cups cake flour
    ¼ tsp. baking powder
    ½ cup milk

Cream together sugar, butter, and shortening. Add eggs one at a time, beating well after each addition. Stir in vanilla. Set aside. Sift together flour and baking powder. Add to creamed mixture alternately with milk, beginning and ending with flour. Beat until smooth. Pour batter into a greased and floured 9-by-5-inch loaf pan. Bake in a 325-degree oven for 1 hour, or until wooden pick inserted in center comes out clean. Remove from oven to cool. *Yields 1 loaf.*

QUICK RED VELVET CAKE

1 box yellow cake mix
1 3-oz. box vanilla instant pudding
2 tbsp. cocoa, sifted
1 cup cooking oil
1 cup water
4 eggs
1 1-oz. bottle red food coloring

Place all ingredients in mixing bowl. Beat with electric mixer for 5 minutes, or until smooth. Pour into three greased and floured 8-inch cake pans. Bake in a 350-degree oven for 25 minutes, or until pick inserted in center comes out clean. Remove from oven. Cool in pan for 10 minutes. Turn out on wire racks to cool. *Yields 10 or more servings.*

ICING

½ cup butter or margarine
8 oz. cream cheese, softened
1 1-lb. box sifted confectioners' sugar

Beat together butter and cream cheese. Add sifted confectioners' sugar. Beat until smooth and creamy. Spread between layers and on top and sides of cool cake.

STRAWBERRY JELLO CAKE

1 box cake mix
1 3-oz. pkg. gelatin
1 cup boiling water
½ cup cold water
1 qt. sliced and sweetened strawberries
1 8-oz. carton whipped topping

Bake cake according to package directions in a 13-by-9-inch pan. Remove from oven and set aside. Mix gelatin with boiling water. Add cold water. Prick cake with fork. Spoon jello over top. Place in refrigerator to cool completely. Serve with fresh, sweetened strawberries and whipped topping. *Yields 12 servings.*

TRIPLE CHOCOLATE CAKE

1 box chocolate butter cake mix
1 3½-oz. pkg. chocolate instant pudding mix
⅔ cup oil
⅔ cup sugar
⅓ cup water
4 eggs
1 cup sour cream
1 cup miniature semi-sweet chocolate chips

Combine cake mix, pudding mix, oil, sugar, and water. Add eggs one at a time, beating well after each addition. Stir in sour cream and chocolate chips. Spoon into a greased and floured 10-inch tube pan. Bake in a 350-degree oven for 1 hour, or until pick inserted in center comes out clean. Remove from oven. Let cool before removing from pan. *Yields 10 to 12 servings.*

TWINKIE CAKE

12 twinkies
1 6-oz. box instant vanilla pudding mix
2 cups mashed and sweetened strawberries
1 15¼-oz. can pineapple tidbits, drained
1 8-oz. container whipped topping
½ cup coconut
1 cup chopped nuts

Cut twinkies in half lengthwise. Place half of twinkies in a 13-by-9-inch pan with the filling-side up. Set aside. Prepare pudding mix by directions on box. Spread half of pudding over twinkies in pan. Add half of strawberries and half of pineapple. Repeat procedure with remaining twinkies, pudding, strawberries, and pineapple. Spread whipped topping over all. Sprinkle with coconut and nuts. Keep refrigerated. *Yields 12 servings.*

VANILLA WAFER CAKE

1 cup butter or margarine, softened
2 cups sugar
6 eggs
3½ cups vanilla wafer crumbs
½ cup milk
2 cups coconut
1 cup chopped nuts

Cream together butter and sugar. Add eggs 2 at a time, beating well after each addition. Mix in half of wafer crumbs. Add milk, then remainder of wafer crumbs. Mix in coconut and nuts. Spoon into a greased and floured 10-inch tube pan. Bake in a 300-degree oven for 1½ hours, or until pick inserted in center comes out clean. Remove from oven to cool. *Yields 10 to 12 servings.*

ICING

⅔ cup sugar
⅔ cup milk
4 tbsp. butter or margarine

Combine all ingredients in a heavy saucepan. Cook over medium heat, stirring constantly to bring to a boil. Boil for 5 minutes. Cool and spread on cake.

YOGURT POUND CAKE

1 cup butter or margarine, softened
1½ cups sugar
3 eggs
2¼ cups all-purpose flour
½ tsp. baking powder
½ tsp. baking soda
½ tsp. salt
1 tsp. grated lemon rind
1 tsp. vanilla
1 8-oz. carton peach yogurt

Cream butter and sugar together. Add eggs one at a time, beating well after each addition. Set aside. Sift together flour, baking powder, baking soda, and salt. Add to creamed mixture. Stir in lemon rind, vanilla, and yogurt. Spoon into a greased and floured 10-inch bundt pan. Bake in a 325-degree oven for 1 hour, or until wooden pick inserted in center comes out clean. Remove from oven. Cool in pan for 15 minutes. Remove to wire rack to cool. *Yields 10 to 12 servings.*

PIES

CITRUS CRUST

The flavors of orange and lemon rinds in this crust make a delectable accompaniment to fruit pies and cobblers.

>3 cups all-purpose flour
>1 tbsp. sugar
>1 tsp. salt
>1 tbsp. grated lemon rind
>2 tsp. grated orange rind
>½ cup butter
>½ cup shortening
>6 to 7 tbsp. ice water

Mix flour, sugar, salt, and rinds together. Cut in butter and shortening with pastry blender or two knives. Add water a little at a time until all flour is moist and mixture sticks together. Roll out on a floured surface to fit desired pie pan or cobbler pan. For a baked crust, prick with fork and bake in a 400-degree oven for 10 to 12 minutes, until brown. *Yields two 9- or 10-inch crusts.*

CREAM CHEESE PASTRY SHELLS

>1 3-oz. pkg. cream cheese, chilled and cubed
>½ cup butter or margarine, chilled and cubed
>1 cup all-purpose flour

With a pastry blender, combine cream cheese and butter. Cut in flour. Form into a ball. Wrap and place in refrigerator to chill for at least 2 hours. When ready to use, shape into 24 balls. Place balls into a greased 1¾-inch muffin pan, pressing into a shell. Bake in a 325-degree oven for 25 to 30 minutes. Spoon in desired filling. *Yields 24 pastry shells.*

FLAKY BUTTER CRUST

1½ cups all-purpose flour
½ tsp. salt
1 tsp. sugar
¼ cup butter or margarine
¼ cup shortening
3 to 4 tbsp. ice water

Sift flour, salt, and sugar into deep bowl. Cut in butter and shortening with pastry blender or two knives until mixture is consistency of coarse meal. Sprinkle water over flour a little at a time, mixing until all is moistened and mixture holds together. Roll out on a lightly floured surface to fit a 9-inch pie pan. For a baked shell, prick with fork and bake in a 400-degree oven for 10 to 12 minutes, until brown. *Yields 1 crust.*

GRAHAM CRACKER CRUST

2 cups graham cracker crumbs
¼ cup sugar
½ cup butter, melted

Combine all ingredients. Press into a 9-inch pan. *Yields one 9-inch crust.*

TART CRUST

½ cup butter, cut into small pieces and chilled
½ cup confectioners' sugar
2 egg yolks
¼ tsp. salt
1¼ cups flour
3 tbsp. ice water

Beat together butter, sugar, and egg yolks. Butter will not mix well, but this is the way it should be. Add salt and half the flour. Stir in half the water, then add remaining flour and water. If dough is too dry, add more water. If too sticky, add more flour. Roll out on a floured surface to fit a 10-inch tart pan.

For a baked crust, preheat oven to 400 degrees. Prick bottom of crust with fork. Bake 10 to 12 minutes, until brown. *Yields one 10-inch crust.*

BROWN SUGAR CHESS PIE

2 eggs
1 cup white sugar
1 cup brown sugar
1 tbsp. flour
1 tbsp. cornmeal
¼ cup milk
¼ cup melted butter
1 tsp. white vinegar
1 tsp. vanilla
1 unbaked 9-inch pie shell

Beat eggs. Set aside. Combine sugars, flour, and cornmeal. Add to eggs. Mix in remaining ingredients. Pour into the unbaked pie shell. Bake in a 350-degree oven for 45 minutes, or until set and brown. *Yields 6 to 8 servings.*

BUTTER PECAN ICE CREAM PIE

**2 cups cold milk
2 3-oz. pkg. vanilla instant pudding
1½ cups butter pecan ice cream, softened
1 9-inch graham cracker pie crust
1 8-oz. carton whipped topping
½ cup chopped pecans**

In a mixing bowl, blend together milk and pudding mix. Stir in ice cream until thoroughly combined. Pour into graham cracker crust. Chill until set. Spread whipped topping on top. Sprinkle with chopped pecans. *Yields 6 to 8 servings.*

Cherry Cream Cheese Pie and Butter Pecan Ice Cream Pie.

CARROT PIE

¾ cup sugar
4 tbsp. butter or margarine, softened
2 tbsp. self-rising flour
3 eggs
1¼ cups evaporated milk
1½ cups grated carrots
½ tsp. cinnamon
½ tsp. vanilla
1 unbaked 9-inch pie crust

Cream together sugar and butter. Stir in flour. Add eggs one at a time, beating well after each addition. Add milk, carrots, cinnamon, and vanilla. Pour into the unbaked pie crust. Bake in a 425-degree oven for 15 minutes. Reduce heat to 350. Bake 30 minutes longer, or until firm. *Yields 6 to 8 servings.*

CHERRY CREAM CHEESE PIE

1 8-oz. pkg. cream cheese, softened
1 14-oz. can sweetened condensed milk
⅓ cup lemon juice
½ tsp. vanilla
1 10-inch graham cracker pie crust
1 21-oz. can cherry pie filling

Beat cream cheese until fluffy. Add condensed milk and beat until smooth. Stir in lemon juice and vanilla. Pour into crust. Chill 3 hours, or until set. Spoon pie filling on top. Keep refrigerated. *Yields 8 servings.*

COCONUT PIES

5 eggs
1 tbsp. flour
2 cups sugar
2 cups coconut
½ cup melted butter or margarine
¾ cup buttermilk
1 tsp. vanilla
2 9-inch unbaked pie shells

In a mixing bowl, beat eggs. Set aside. Mix together flour and sugar, then add to beaten eggs. Stir in coconut, melted butter, buttermilk, and vanilla. Pour into pie crusts. Bake in a 350-degree oven for 40 to 45 minutes, until set and brown on top. *Yields 2 pies.*

HEAVENLY FRUIT PIE

1 14-oz. can sweetened condensed milk
1 12-oz. carton whipped topping
1 15¼-oz. can crushed pineapple, drained
1 11-oz. can mandarin oranges, drained
⅓ cup lemon juice
½ cup chopped pecans
2 9-inch graham cracker pie crusts

Combine all ingredients except pie crusts. Stir well. Pour into pie crusts. Chill several hours before serving. *Yields 2 pies.*

KEY LIME PIE

1 cup sugar
¼ cup self-rising flour
3 tbsp. cornstarch
2 cups water
3 egg yolks
3 tbsp. butter or margarine
¼ cup fresh lime juice
Grated rind of 1 lime
Dash green food coloring
1 baked 9-inch pie shell

Combine sugar, flour, and cornstarch in a heavy saucepan. Slowly stir in water. Cook, stirring constantly until thickened, about 8 minutes. Gradually stir some of mixture into beaten egg yolks. Return to saucepan, mixing all together. Cook, stirring for about 2 additional minutes. Remove from heat. Mix in butter, lime juice, rind, and food coloring. Cool. Pour into cool baked crust. Make meringue while filling cools.

MERINGUE

3 egg whites
¼ tsp. cream of tartar
6 tbsp. sugar

Beat egg whites until frothy, but not stiff. Add cream of tartar and continue to beat until stiff. Gradually beat in sugar. Beat until stiff and glossy. Spread on pie filling until it touches edges of crust. Bake in a 400-degree oven until brown, about 10 minutes. *Yields 6 to 8 servings.*

LEMON ICEBOX PIE

2 cups vanilla wafer crumbs
2 dozen whole vanilla wafers
1 14-oz. can sweetened condensed milk
2 eggs, separated
⅓ cup lemon juice
4 tbsp. sugar
½ tsp. vanilla

Pat crumbs evenly into bottom of a 9-inch pie pan. Stand whole wafers up around sides of pan, overlapping them as you go.

Mix together condensed milk, 2 beaten egg yolks, and lemon juice. Beat until smooth. Pour into the vanilla wafer pie crust. Set aside. Beat 2 egg whites until stiff. Add sugar and vanilla. Beat until well blended. Spread on top of pie filling. Bake in a 350-degree oven for 10 to 12 minutes, until meringue is brown. Remove from oven and place in refrigerator to cool before serving. *Yields 6 to 8 servings.*

LEMONADE PIE

1 14-oz. can sweetened condensed milk
1 6-oz. can frozen lemonade, thawed
1 8-oz. container whipped topping
1 9-inch graham cracker pie crust

Combine condensed milk, lemonade, and whipped topping. Pour into graham cracker crust. Chill for at least 2 hours before serving. *Yields 6 to 8 servings.*

PINEAPPLE PIE

1 8-oz. pkg. cream cheese, softened
1 14-oz. can sweetened condensed milk
⅓ cup lemon juice
1 20-oz. can crushed pineapple, drained
1 9-inch graham cracker pie crust
1 8-oz. carton whipped topping

Beat together cream cheese, condensed milk, and lemon juice. Stir in pineapple. Pour into the graham cracker crust. Chill for several hours. When ready to serve, top with whipped topping. *Yields 6 to 8 servings.*

PLUM GOOD PIE

1 cup plus 2 tsp. sugar
2 tbsp. cornstarch
½ tsp. cinnamon
5 cups chopped and seeded plums
Pastry for 2-crust pie
¼ cup melted butter or margarine

Mix together 1 cup sugar, cornstarch, and cinnamon. Stir in plums. Spoon into unbaked pie shell. Pour all but 1 tablespoon butter over plums. Place top crust over plum filling. Make slits in crust. Brush with remaining tablespoon butter. Sprinkle with 2 teaspoons sugar. Bake in a 350-degree oven for 1 hour, or until crust is brown. *Yields 6 to 8 servings.*

PUMPKIN PIE

1 cup strained pumpkin
½ cup evaporated milk or cream
2 eggs, beaten
1 tbsp. butter, melted
¾ cup sugar
¼ tsp. cinnamon
¼ tsp. allspice
1 9-inch unbaked pie shell

Place all ingredients except pie shell in a blender. Blend until smooth. Pour into the pie shell. Bake in a 450-degree oven for 15 minutes. Reduce heat to 350 and bake 30 to 35 minutes longer, until firm and very brown. *Yields 6 to 8 servings.*

RHUBARB PIE

2½ cups sugar
1⅓ cups water
5 cups rhubarb, cut in 1-inch pieces
6 tbsp. cornstarch
1 baked 9-inch pie shell
1 cup whipping cream, whipped

Mix together sugar and 1 cup water in a heavy saucepan. Bring to a boil, stirring to dissolve sugar. Add rhubarb. Cook, stirring occasionally, until rhubarb is softened, about 10 minutes. Remove rhubarb from syrup with a slotted spoon. Set aside. Blend cornstarch with remaining ⅓ cup water. Add to boiling syrup. Cook, stirring, until thick and clear, about 5 minutes. Add rhubarb. Remove from heat. Cool 5 minutes. Pour into the pie shell. Cool completely. Top with whipped cream to serve. *Yields 6 to 8 servings.*

VINEGAR COBBLER PIE

⅔ cup shortening
2 cups self-rising flour
⅓ cup ice water
2 cups sugar
3 tbsp. flour
½ cup butter
1 qt. water
⅔ cup white vinegar

Place shortening and 2 cups flour in a mixing bowl. Blend in shortening with a pastry blender. Add ice water gradually to moisten. On a floured surface, roll out two-thirds of the dough. Cut into strips. Place half of the strips on bottom of an 8-by-12-inch bread pan that will hold 2 quarts.

Mix sugar and 3 tablespoons flour together. Spinkle half over dough strips. Dot with half of butter. Place another layer of dough strips over sugar mixture. Sprinkle with remaining sugar. Dot with remaining butter.

Roll out the remaining third of dough to fit over top of pan. Cut in half. Lay one half, then the other half, leaving a slight crack in center where crusts meet. Set aside. Mix 1 quart water and vinegar together. Heat until just hot, about 5 minutes. Pour vinegar-water mixture over crust. Bake in a 350-degree oven for about 1 hour, until brown. *Yields 10 to 12 servings.*

STORIES

SICK HUMOR

"A merry heart doeth good like a medicine." It's in the Bible! I read a scientist's report saying laughter stimulates a part of the brain, relieving stress, anxiety, and fear, therefore allowing the immune system to work better. The following stories prove this to be true.

JUST STAY OFF THE TRACKS

An explosion caused Willie's brother, Dude, to be severely burned. While in the hospital, he was hallucinating, but he knew the images he was seeing were not really there. He didn't know if the hallucinations were caused from the pain and swelling, the medicine, or if he was simply losing his mind.

One day he was expressing his fears to Willie, when he said, "I know this can't be, but right now as I look out into the hallway, I imagine I see a train goin' by. Is that anything to be concerned about?"

Willie said, "No, I don't think so, as long as it don't run over ya."

This gave Dude a big laugh and he thinks it helped him get well. He said every time he began to dwell on how sick he was and feel sorry for himself, he would think of the train and laugh. For Dude, laughter really was the best medicine.

THE MOST WONDERFUL SURPRISE OF ALL

With Willie being a diabetic, we were elated each time the test tape showed no green, which meant his sugar was under control.

He would often go off his diet, thinking if he could hide a forbidden treat from me it would do him no harm.

Once, when leaving to go away for a few days, I cautioned him to be sure to stay on his diet. I said, "Please don't go to the store and get candy and ice cream!" He assured me he wouldn't.

When I returned, Willie met me at the door with excitement in his voice, and said, "Do I have a surprise for you!" and disappeared into the bathroom. I had visions of diamonds, perfume, or at least a new toaster or electric fry pan. It had to be small, for when he emerged from the bathroom, his hand was behind his back. It was an exciting moment as he slowly pulled his hand from behind his back, and said, "Ta-da!", pushing a test tape showing no green under my nose. I'm sure the sparkle in my eyes did not match the sparkle and excitement in his; however, I recovered quickly and rewarded him with a hug, telling him how proud I was of him. He had been a good boy.

IS YOUR GUN JAMMED?

One Sunday morning, while working at a nursing home, Clara was wheeling Mrs. Hanks down the hall to church services. She was dressed in her Sunday best. Her snow-white hair was fixed in the latest style. She had on jewelry and lipstick and was as cute as could be. Even though she was crippled and almost blind, she still had a wonderful sense of humor. Clara felt it a real pleasure to do little things for her.

This particular morning, she was urging Clara to hurry and exclaimed, "If I could just get out of this chair and walk, I wouldn't be late."

Clara told her they had plenty of time, and said, "You know, Mrs. Hanks, you're a pistol."

She replied, "I may be, honey, but it's been a long time since I fired."

YOU CAN HAVE 'EM!

After suffering with a toothache for some time, Dude went to the dentist. He said, "Doc, I'm having such pain, I just want all my teeth pulled and dentures made."

After examining his teeth, the dentist said, "Dude, I think I can save your teeth."

Dude replied, "You just go ahead and pull 'em out and save 'em if you want to, Doc. I don't want 'em!"

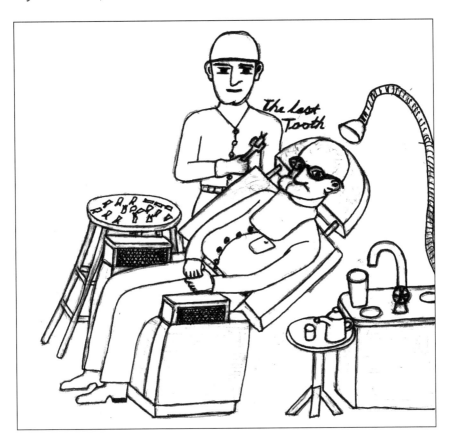

STORIES • 173

IT MATTERS NOT THE NAME

A nurse came into Mama's hospital room with a hypodermic needle in her hand. She said, "Are you Mrs. Lock?"

Mama answered, "Naw, my name's Mud."

The nurse smiled sweetly and said, "Well, the doctor told me if Mrs. Lock wasn't in here to give this shot to Mrs. Mud."

NOT SO "WELL-DONE"

Theo liked his eggs well-done, but he had been very sick and his diet called for poached eggs.

One day, Margaret brought in his breakfast tray containing two poached eggs and a piece of toast. After arranging his tray, she suddenly realized there was no juice. She said, "Oh, I forgot your drink!"

Theo replied, "Oh, that's okay. I'll just drink these eggs."

Cookies, Candies, and Other Desserts

With Stories from Religion's Funny Side

Cream Cheese Cookies, No-Bake Brownies, Pecan Sandies, Date Balls, and Danish Wedding Cookies.

HELPFUL HINTS

• When bananas start to get old, make banana bread, banana pudding, use them in jello, or fry them.
• Use a collar made from foil for funnel cakes to make them uniform.

COOKIES

ALMOND COOKIES

2 eggs
1 cup sugar
½ cup butter, melted and cooled
¼ tsp. almond extract
4 cups flour
1 tsp. baking soda
1 tsp. baking powder
1 cup sour cream

Beat eggs and sugar together. Add butter and extract. Set aside. Sift flour, soda, and baking powder together. Add to egg-sugar mixture along with sour cream. Chill for at least 2 hours.

When ready to bake, roll out on floured surface. Cut into 2½-inch circles. Place on greased cookie sheet. Bake in a 350-degree oven for 12 to 15 minutes. *Yields about 3 dozen cookies.*

CREAM CHEESE COOKIES

A chewy cookie that is so pretty.

1 8-oz. pkg. cream cheese, softened
¼ cup butter or margarine, softened
1 egg
¼ tsp. vanilla
1 box butter recipe cake mix
Pecan halves

Mix cream cheese and butter together. Add egg and vanilla. Beat until smooth. Stir in cake mix. Place in refrigerator for at least 1 hour. Remove from refrigerator and roll into small balls about the size of a walnut. Place 2 inches apart on greased cookie sheet. Push a pecan half into top of each ball. Bake at 350 degrees for 8 to 10 minutes. *Yields about 6 dozen.*

CRISPY OATMEALS

1½ cups brown sugar
¾ cup margarine, melted
⅓ cup buttermilk
½ tsp. vanilla
1½ cups self-rising flour
¼ tsp. baking soda
3 cups oats

Cream together brown sugar and margarine. Add buttermilk and vanilla. Set aside. Sift flower and baking soda together. Stir into brown sugar mixture. Stir in oats. Place in refrigerator for at least 1 hour.

Grease 2 cookie sheets. Roll dough into 1-inch balls. Place on cookie sheets 2 inches apart. Flatten with glass that has been dipped in cold water. Bake in a 375-degree oven for about 10 minutes, or until edges of cookies begin to brown. *Yields about 5 dozen.*

DANISH WEDDING COOKIES

These cookies literally melt in your mouth and are so easy to make. They contain no eggs, salt, or baking powder.

2 tbsp. sugar
½ cup margarine, softened
1 cup all-purpose flour
1 tsp. vanilla
1 cup finely chopped nuts
⅓ cup sifted confectioners' sugar
¼ tsp. allspice

Beat together sugar and margarine. Add flour. Stir in vanilla and nuts. Mix well with hands. Roll into small balls. Place on a greased cookie sheet. Bake in a 350-degree oven for 20 minutes. Remove from oven. Set aside. Mix confectioners' sugar and allspice together. While cookies are warm, roll in confectioners' sugar mixture. *Yields about 3 dozen.*

DATE BALLS

The Rice Krispies cereal makes this a delicious, crunchy cookie.

½ cup melted margarine, cooled
1 8-oz. pkg. pitted dates, chopped
1 cup brown sugar
1 egg, beaten
2 cups Rice Krispies cereal
1 cup chopped nuts
1 tsp. vanilla
½ cup shredded coconut

In a heavy saucepan, mix margarine, dates, brown sugar, and egg. Cook over medium heat for about 5 to 8 minutes, stirring constantly until mixture is thick and dates are dissolved. Remove from heat. Let cool for 10 minutes. Stir in cereal, nuts, and vanilla. With buttered hands, roll teaspoonfuls of mixture into balls. Roll balls in coconut. *Yields about 4 dozen.*

GRAHAM CRACKER CRISPS

These bars need to be taken off the cookie sheet and put on racks to cool immediately after removing from the oven, or they will stick to the pan. They seem messy, but are delicious and crunchy like a crispy wafer cookie.

12 double graham crackers
1 cup butter or margarine, melted
1 cup brown sugar
1 cup chopped nuts

Line cookie sheet or jelly roll pan with graham crackers. Set aside. In a heavy saucepan, mix together melted butter, brown sugar, and chopped nuts. Cook over medium heat while stirring until mixture comes to a boil. Boil for 2 minutes. Remove from heat. Pour and spread over crackers. Bake in a 350-degree oven for 10 minutes. When bubbly, remove from oven. Cut and lift out while still hot. Yields 24 servings.

ORANGE REFRIGERATOR COOKIES

1 cup butter or margarine, softened
½ cup white sugar
½ cup light brown sugar
1 egg
2 tbsp. orange juice
¼ tsp. vanilla
2½ cups flour
¼ tsp. salt
¼ tsp. baking soda
1 tbsp. grated orange peel
½ cup chopped nuts

In a mixing bowl, cream together butter and sugars. Beat in egg, orange juice, and vanilla. Set aside. Sift together flour, salt, and soda; then stir into butter-sugar mixture. Stir in peel and nuts. Chill until easy to handle, about 1 hour.

On wax paper, shape into two 1¼-inch diameter rolls. Wrap in wax paper and refrigerate until firm, 3 to 4 hours. Slice thin, about ¼ inch. Place on ungreased cookie sheets. Bake in a 375-degree oven for about 8 minutes, or until they begin to brown around edges. Remove to wire racks to cool. *Yields about 10 dozen.*

Note: I ususally bake one roll and leave the other in the refrigerator for a later date. It will keep in the refrigerator for up to a week; in freezer up to three months. If frozen, thaw before slicing.

PEANUT BUTTER KISS COOKIES

¾ cup butter or margarine
1 cup creamy peanut butter
½ cup brown sugar
½ cup white sugar
2 eggs, beaten
2½ cups all-purpose flour
½ tsp. baking powder
¼ tsp. salt
About 48 swirl-top chocolate kisses

Cream together butter, peanut butter, and sugars. Beat in eggs. Set aside. Sift together dry ingredients. Add to creamed mixture. Refrigerate dough for at least 1 hour. When ready to bake, shape dough into 1-inch balls. Place 2 inches apart on ungreased cookie sheets. Bake in a 375-degree oven for 10 to 12 minutes. Remove from oven and immediately press kiss down in middle of each cookie so that cookie cracks around edges. Remove to racks to cool. *Yields about 4 dozen.*

PARTY PASTELS

2 cups butter, softened
2 cups sifted confectioners' sugar
4½ cups flour
½ tsp. salt

Cream together butter and sugar. Set aside. Sift flour with salt. Add flour to creamed mixture a little at a time. Use hands to mix if necessary. If dough is too dry, add 1 or 2 tablespoons cream. Divide dough into fourths. Add food coloring and flavoring combinations listed below. Mold each into a roll about 2 inches in diameter. Wrap in plastic wrap and refrigerate for several hours or overnight. To bake, slice ⅛-inch thick. Place on an ungreased cookie sheet. Bake in a 375-degree oven for 7 to 9 minutes. Do not brown. *Yields about 10 dozen cookies.*

GREEN COOKIES

2 tbsp. grated lemon rind
3 drops green food coloring

YELLOW COOKIES

2 tbsp. grated orange rind
3 drops yellow food coloring
½ cup finely chopped nuts

PINK COOKIES

3 drops red food coloring
¼ cup red crystal sugars

CHOCOLATE COOKIES

2 quares of semisweet baking chocolate, melted
¼ cup chocolate shot

PECAN SANDIES

1 cup butter flavored shortening
½ cup sifted confectioners' sugar
½ cup granulated sugar
¼ tsp. salt
1 egg
1 tsp. vanilla
½ cup finely chopped pecans
2½ cups all-purpose flour
½ tsp. baking soda
½ tsp. cream of tartar

Beat together shortening, sugars, and salt until creamy. Add egg and vanilla. Beat until light and fluffy. Stir in pecans. Set aside. Sift together flour, soda, and cream of tartar. Stir into creamed mixture. Chill dough for about 2 hours. Shape dough into balls the size of a walnut. Place on an ungreased cookie sheet about 2 inches apart. Press flat with fingers. Bake in a 350-degree oven for 10 to 12 minutes. These cookies aren't necessarily brown when done. *Yields about 4 dozen.*

UNCOOKED FRUIT ROLL

1 1-lb. bag vanilla wafers
2 cups chopped nuts
2 cups candied fruit
1 14-oz. can condensed milk

Crush vanilla wafers into fine crumbs. Add remaining ingredients. Mix with hands if necessary. Shape into two long rolls. Wrap in wax paper and refrigerate. Slice when ready to serve. *Yields about 4 dozen slices.*

CANDIES

BON-BONS

1 1-lb. box sifted confectioners' sugar
1 14-oz. pkg. coconut
1 14-oz. can sweetened condensed milk
1 tsp. vanilla
3 cups pecans, chopped
1 12-oz. pkg. semisweet chocolate chips
1½ sticks (slabs) Gulf paraffin wax

Mix first five ingredients together. Shape into small balls. Place on cookie sheet and put in freezer for 2 hours. In double boiler over boiling water, melt chocolate chips and paraffin wax. Dip each frozen ball in chocolate mixture, using tongs. Place on wax paper to harden. *Yields about 3 dozen.*

EASY CHEESY FUDGE

1 cup margarine, melted
8 oz. Velveeta cheese
1 tsp. vanilla
2 lb. sifted confectioners' sugar
½ cup sifted cocoa
½ cup chopped nuts

In a microwave or heavy saucepan, melt and beat together margarine and cheese. Remove from heat. Add vanilla, sugar, and cocoa. Beat until creamy and smooth. Add nuts. Pour into a buttered 9-by-9-inch square pan. Cool and cut into squares. *Yields 2½ pounds.*

FABULOUS FUDGE

2½ cups sugar
¾ cup evaporated milk
1 cup marshmallow cream
¼ cup butter or margarine
¼ tsp. salt
1 6-oz. pkg. semisweet chocolate chips
1 tsp. vanilla
1 cup chopped nuts

In a heavy saucepan, combine first five ingredients. Over medium heat, bring to a boil, stirring constantly. Cook for 5 minutes, continuing to stir. Remove from heat. Stir in chocolate chips and vanilla. Beat until chips are melted and mixture is smooth. Add nuts. Spread in a buttered 8-inch square pan. Cool and cut into 2-inch squares. *Yields 16 squares.*

MICROWAVE PEANUT BRITTLE

1 cup sugar
½ cup light syrup
1 cup raw peanuts
¼ tsp. salt
1 tbsp. butter
1 tsp. vanilla
1 tsp. baking soda

Combine sugar, syrup, peanuts, and salt in a 2-quart casserole. Place in microwave on high for 5 minutes. Remove from oven and stir. Place back in oven. Cook on high for 5 minutes more. Remove. Mixture should be a light brown color. Add butter and vanilla, blending thoroughly. Microwave on high for 3 minutes longer, or until mixture reaches hard stage (300 degrees on candy thermometer). Remove from oven and add soda, stirring to combine. Spread out on greased cookie sheet. Let cool. Break into serving pieces. *Yields about 1 pound.*

MINTS

1 3-oz. pkg. cream cheese, softened
½ tsp. peppermint extract
3 cups sifted confectioners' sugar
3 to 4 drops food coloring of your choice

In a mixing bowl, beat cream cheese until creamy. Add extract, confectioners' sugar, and food coloring. Beat until smooth, kneading in the last of the sugar by hand. Roll into balls about the size of a walnut. Place on wax paper. Flatten with fork. *Yields about 3 dozen.*

Easy Cheesy Fudge and Mints.

PEANUT BUTTER FUDGE

**2 cups sugar
2 tbsp. white syrup
⅛ tsp. salt
¼ cup margarine
¾ cup sweet milk
⅓ cup peanut butter
1 tsp. vanilla**

Mix together first five ingredients in a large saucepan. Cook to soft-ball stage, 10 to 15 minutes. Remove from heat. Add peanut butter and vanilla. Beat until mixture begins to thicken. Pour into a buttered 9-inch square pan. Cool and cut into 2-inch squares. *Yields about 16 squares.*

WHITE CHOCOLATE FUDGE

**2 cups sugar
¾ cup sour cream
½ cup butter or margarine, softened
14 oz. white chocolate, broken
 into small pieces
½ tsp. vanilla
1 7-oz. jar marshmallow cream
1 cup candied cherries, chopped**

In a heavy saucepan, combine sugar, sour cream, and butter. Bring mixture to a boil, stirring constantly. Boil for 7 minutes, continuing to stir. Remove from heat. Stir in white chocolate until it is completely melted. Add vanilla and marshmallow cream. Beat until thoroughly combined. Add candied cherries. Pour into a buttered 9-inch square pan. Cool and cut into 2-inch squares. *Yields about 16 squares.*

SUCKERS

You will need a candy thermometer and candy molds to make these.

Vegetable oil
1 cup sugar
⅓ cup hot water
⅓ cup light corn syrup
½ tsp. orange, lemon, or flavoring of your choice
½ tsp. food color of your choice

Brush molds lightly with vegetable oil. Combine sugar, water, and corn syrup in a heavy saucepan. Place on high heat, stirring with a wooden spoon until all sugar is dissolved, scraping sugar down from sides of pan. Clip thermometer on side of pan and continue cooking without stirring until thermometer reaches 300 degrees, about 10 minutes. Remove from heat.

Let stand until bubbles disappear. Add flavoring and food color. Stir to blend. Pour into prepared molds. Let harden at room temperature for about 10 minutes. Unmold hardened candy by inverting and gently flexing molds. *Makes 10 small suckers.*

OTHER DESSERTS

APPLE PEACH BETTY

1 29-oz. can sliced peaches, drained (save juice to use another time)
1 21-oz. can apple pie filling
1 tbsp. grated lemon peel
½ tsp. allspice
1 cup all-purpose flour
½ cup sugar
½ cup butter or margarine
¾ cup chopped nuts
Ice cream

Mix first four ingredients together in a deep 9-by-9-inch baking dish. Set aside.

Mix together flour and sugar. Cut in butter with a pastry blender until mixture is like coarse crumbs. Add ½ cup chopped nuts. Spoon over apple-peach mixture in pan. Bake in a 425-degree oven for 15 minutes. Remove from oven and sprinkle remaining nuts on top. Return to the oven for 5 to 10 minutes longer, or until top is brown and filling is bubbly. Serve warm with ice cream. *Yields 8 servings.*

APPLE RINGS

2 medium-sized apples
1 cup water
2 cups sugar
⅓ cup red cinnamon candies
Few drops red food coloring

Peel and core apples, leaving them whole. Slice into ½-inch slices. Set aside. Mix together the water, sugar, candies, and food coloring in a saucepan. Bring mixture to a boil. Drop in apple rings. Simmer until tender, about 10 minutes. Remove from syrup. Serve as an accompaniment to ham or chicken. *Yields 8 to 10 apple rings.*

CARAMEL APPLES

1 14-oz. pkg. caramel kisses
2 tbsp. water
⅛ tsp. salt
6 unpeeled medium-sized apples
1 cup finely chopped nuts

Place caramels, water, and salt in top of double boiler over boiling water until caramels are melted and mixture is smooth, about 10 minutes. Stick wooden skewer in blossom end of apples. Dip in caramel. Sprinkle with nuts. Set on wax paper-lined cookie sheet. If caramel becomes too stiff add a few drops of water. Chill until caramel coating is firm. *Yields enough for 6 apples.*

BAKED APPLES-FOURS WITH HARD SAUCE

4 baking apples
¼ cup sugar
¼ cup butter or margarine
¼ cup light corn syrup
¼ tsp. cinnamon

Core apples, leaving whole, and peel one-fourth down from stem. Place in baking dish. In a small saucepan, combine remaining ingredients. Bring to a boil. Pour over apples. Bake in a 350-degree oven for 45 minutes, or until apples are tender. Serve warm topped with hard sauce. *Yields 4 servings.*

HARD SAUCE

⅓ cup butter or margarine
1 cup confectioners' sugar
¼ tsp. rum extract

Beat together butter and sugar until smooth. Beat in rum extract. Serve over warm apples. *Yields about 1 cup.*

BLUSHING PEACHES

About 10 peaches, peeled and sliced
1 cup sugar
2 tbsp. strawberry gelatin

Place peaches in a heavy saucepan. Mix sugar and gelatin together. Pour over peaches. Mix thoroughly. Place over medium heat and bring to a boil. Boil gently for about 10 minutes, until peaches are just tender. Cool. Eat as is, or serve over shortcake or topped with whipped cream. *Yields 6 servings.*

BUTTERNUT BARS

2 eggs
½ cup butter, softened
2 cups firmly packed brown sugar
1 tsp. vanilla
1½ cups self-rising flour
1 cup chopped nuts

Beat eggs. Add butter, sugar, and vanilla. Beat until smooth. Stir in flour and nuts. Pour into a well-greased and floured 13-by-9-inch baking pan. Bake in a 350-degree oven for 25 to 30 minutes, or until brown. Cut into bars. *Yields 12 to 16 bars.*

CAKE MIX BARS

1 pkg. yellow cake mix, with pudding in mix
⅓ cup butter or margarine, softened
3 eggs
1 cup chopped nuts
1 6-oz. pkg. semisweet chocolate chips
1 14-oz. can sweetened condensed milk
1 tsp. vanilla

Mix together cake mix, butter, and 1 egg. Beat with mixer until crumbly. Press evenly into a greased 13-by-9-inch baking pan. Bake in a 350-degree oven for 15 minutes. Remove from oven. Sprinkle nuts and chocolate chips over top. Set aside. Beat 2 eggs and condensed milk together. Add vanilla. Pour over nuts and chocolate chips. Bake in a 350-degree oven for 25 to 30 minutes, or until center is set. Cool and cut into bars. *Yields 12 to 16 bars.*

CARAMEL SAUCE

1¼ cups brown sugar
⅔ cup light corn syrup
¼ cup butter
½ cup heavy cream
½ tsp. vanilla
½ cup chopped nuts

Thoroughly mix together sugar and corn syrup in a heavy saucepan. Cook over medium heat to soft-ball stage, 236 degrees on candy thermometer. Remove from heat. Add butter, cream, vanilla, and nuts. Great served hot over ice cream or cake. Store any leftover sauce in the refrigerator. Reheat if desired. *Yields about 2 cups.*

CHOCOLATE CUPCAKES

⅓ cup shortening
1 cup sugar
1 egg
2 cups self-rising flour
¾ cup milk
1 tsp. vanilla
1 6-oz. pkg. semisweet mini-chocolate chips
½ cup chopped nuts

Cream together shortening and sugar. Beat in egg. Add flour alternately with milk. Stir in vanilla, chocolate chips, and nuts. Bake in greased and floured muffin pans in a 375-degree oven for 20 minutes. *Yields about 16 cupcakes.*

CHERRY CHEESE BARS

1¼ cups self-rising flour
½ cup firmly packed brown sugar
½ cup butter flavored shortening
1 cup nuts, chopped and divided in half
½ cup flaked coconut
1 8-oz. pkg. cream cheese, softened
⅓ cup sugar
1 egg
1 tsp. vanilla
1 21-oz. can cherry pie filling

Combine flour and brown sugar. Cut in shortening with pastry blender. Add fi cup nuts and the coconut. Remove half of mixture and set aside. Press remaining crumbs in bottom of a greased 13-by-9-inch pan. Bake in a 350-degree oven for 12 to 15 minutes, until edges are lightly browned. Remove from oven and set aside.

Beat together cream cheese, sugar, egg, and vanilla. Spread over hot baked crust. Return to oven for 10 minutes. Remove from oven. Spread cherry pie filling over cream cheese. Sprinkle reserved crumbs and the remaining nuts over cherries. Return to oven. Bake 15 minutes longer. Cool and cut into bars. *Yields 12 to 16 bars.*

CHOCOLATE PEANUT BUTTER BARS

FILLING

¼ cup butter or margarine
1½ cups peanut butter
1¼ cups confectioners' sugar
1 tsp. vanilla
¾ cup chopped pecans

Cream together butter and peanut butter. Add sugar and vanilla. Beat until smooth. Stir in pecans. Set aside.

CRUST

1½ cups self-rising flour
⅔ cup brown sugar
⅔ cup butter or margarine, softened
2 egg yolks, beaten
1 tsp. vanilla
1 11½-oz. pkg. milk chocolate chips

Mix flour and sugar together. Cut in margarine with a pastry blender. Add egg yolks and vanilla. Press into bottom of an ungreased 13-by-9-inch baking pan. Bake in a 350-degree oven for 12 to 15 minutes, until golden brown. Remove from oven. Turn oven off. Spread filling on crust. Sprinkle with the chocolate chips. Return to oven for a few minutes, until chips are softened. Remove from oven and spread chocolate. Cool and cut into bars. *Yields 12 to 16 bars.*

CHOCOLATE SAUCE

2 cups sugar
2 squares unsweetened chocolate, cut in small pieces
¼ cup light corn syrup
¾ cup water
⅛ tsp. salt
2 tbsp. butter
1 tsp. vanilla
1 cup chopped nuts

In a heavy saucepan, mix together sugar, chocolate, corn syrup, water, and salt. Place over medium heat and cook to soft-ball stage, 236 degrees on candy thermometer. Remove from heat. Add butter, vanilla, and nuts. Delicious served hot over ice cream or cake. *Yields about 2 cups.*

COCONUT PECAN BARS

1 cup butter or margarine
2 cups brown sugar, firmly packed
2 eggs
1 tsp. vanilla
2 cups self-rising flour
1 3½-oz. can coconut
1 cup chopped pecans
Sifted confectioners' sugar

Cream butter and sugar together. Add eggs and vanilla, beating well. Stir in flour, coconut, and pecans. Spread in a buttered 15-by-10-inch jelly-roll pan. Bake in a 350-degree oven for about 25 minutes, or until done. Remove from oven to cool. Sprinkle confectioners' sugar on top. Cut into 2-inch bars to serve. *Yields about 35 bars.*

FRIED APPLES

6 large cooking apples
¼ cup butter or margarine
2 tbsp. lemon juice
¼ tsp. salt
⅔ cup sugar
½ tsp. cinnamon
⅛ tsp. nutmeg
2 tbsp. water

Peel and core apples. Cut into quarters, then cut quarters in half. Melt butter in heavy skillet. Add apples. Sprinkle with lemon juice and salt. Mix sugar and spices together. Stir into apples. Sprinkle water over all. Cover skillet and cook over medium heat, stirring often until apples are tender, about 15 minutes. Remove from heat. Serve with ham or pork roast as a side dish, or for dessert with whipped cream or ice cream. *Yields 4 to 6 servings.*

FRIED BANANAS

This is a great dessert for diabetics. If the bananas used are very ripe, no sugar is needed.

¼ cup butter or margarine
4 very ripe bananas

In a heavy skillet, melt butter. Add sliced bananas. Cook over low heat for 5 to 10 minutes. *Yields 6 servings.*

HOT FUDGE SUNDAE DESSERT

1 12-oz. pkg. vanilla wafers, crushed
½ cup finely chopped pecans
¾ cup butter or margarine, melted
½ gallon ice cream, softened

Combine crumbs, pecans, and butter, mixing well. Press half of mixture into a 13-by-9-inch dish. Spread ice cream evenly over crust. Press remaining crumb mixture over ice cream. Cover. Freeze until firm. To serve, cut in squares and top each serving with hot fudge sauce. *Yields 12 to 16 servings.*

HOT FUDGE SAUCE

1 cup sugar
3 tbsp. all-purpose flour
¼ cup plus 1 tbsp. cocoa
1 cup milk
2 tbsp. butter
1 tsp. vanilla

Sift together sugar, flour, and cocoa. Combine in saucepan with milk. Cook over medium heat, stirring constantly until thickened, about 5 minutes. Remove from heat. Add butter and vanilla. Stir until smooth. *Yields about 2 cups.*

LAYERED BARS

1½ cups graham cracker crumbs
¾ cup sugar
⅓ cup margarine, melted
1 8-oz. pkg. cream cheese
1 egg
¾ cup flaked coconut
1 cup chopped nuts
1 6-oz. pkg. semisweet chocolate chips

Mix together cracker crumbs, ¼ cup sugar, and margarine. Press into bottom of a 13-by-9-inch baking pan. Bake in a 350-degree oven for 5 minutes. Remove from oven and set aside. Combine cream cheese, fi cup sugar, and egg until well blended. Spread over crust. Sprinkle with layer of coconut, nuts, and chocolate chips. Bake in a 350-degree oven for 25 to 30 minutes, or until brown. Cool and cut into bars. *Yields 12 to 16 bars.*

LEMON CREAM CHEESE CRESCENT KNOTS

1 3-oz. pkg. cream cheese, softened
¼ cup sugar
1 tsp. grated lemon rind
2 tsp. plus 1 tbsp. lemon juice
2 8-oz. cans refrigerated crescent rolls
½ cup sifted confectioners' sugar

Combine cream cheese, sugar, lemon rind, and 2 teaspoons lemon juice. Set aside. Separate rolls into 8 rectangles. Press perforations together to seal. Spread 2 teaspoons cream cheese mixture over each rectangle. Roll up jelly-roll fashion, starting at long end. Stretch dough carefully and just slightly. Tie in a loose knot. Place on a lightly buttered baking sheet. Bake in a 350-degree oven for about 20 minutes, until golden brown. Combine confectioners' sugar and 1 tablespoon lemon juice. Drizzle over rolls. *Serves 8.*

MAGIC COOKIE BARS

½ cup butter or margarine, melted
1½ cups graham cracker crumbs
1 14-oz. can sweetened condensed milk
1 6-oz. pkg. semisweet chocolate chips
1 cup chopped nuts

Mix together melted butter and graham cracker crumbs. Press into a 13-by-9-inch baking pan. Pour milk evenly over crumbs. Top evenly with chocolate chips and nuts. Press down with spatula. Bake in a 350-degree oven for 25 minutes, or until brown. Cool before cutting into squares. *Yields 12 to 16 squares.*

Note: To make Rainbow Cookie Bars, substitute 1 cup M & M's plain chocolate candies for the chocolate chips.

NO-BAKE BROWNIES

These brownies are similar to fudge candy, and a family favorite.

1 cup evaporated milk
2 cups miniature marshmallows
1 cup semisweet chocolate chips
⅓ cup sugar
⅛ tsp. salt
1 tbsp. butter
½ tsp. vanilla
3 cups graham cracker crumbs
½ cup nuts, chopped

Mix together milk, marshmallows, chocolate chips, sugar, and salt in heavy saucepan. Bring to a boil, stirring constantly. Boil for 5 minutes. Remove from heat. Add butter, vanilla, cracker crumbs, and nuts. Pack into a 9-inch square pan. Refrigerate to harden. Cut into 2-inch squares. *Yields about 16 squares.*

PEACHY YAM BAKE

½ cup firmly packed brown sugar
3 tbsp. flour
½ tsp. nutmeg
2 tbsp. butter or margarine
½ cup chopped nuts
2 17-oz. cans yams, drained
1 16-oz. can peach slices, drained
1½ cups miniature marshmallows

Combine brown sugar, flour, and nutmeg. Cut in butter with a pastry blender. Add nuts. Set aside. Arrange yams and peaches in a 3-quart casserole. Sprinkle with sugar mixture. Bake in a 350-degree oven for 35 minutes. Remove and sprinkle with marshmallows. Return to oven for 5 to 10 minutes, until marshmallows are melted and brown. *Yields 8 to 10 servings.*

PEANUT BUTTER AND JELLY BARS

3 cups self-rising flour
1 cup sugar
½ cup butter or margarine, softened
½ cup peanut butter
2 eggs, beaten
1 cup grape jelly

Combine flour and sugar. Cut in butter and peanut butter with pastry blender. Stir in eggs, mixing well. Press half of mixture into a greased 13-by-9-inch pan. Spread jelly over mixture in pan. Crumble remaining mixture over jelly. Bake in a 350-degree oven for 30 to 35 minutes. Cool and cut into bars. *Yields 12 to 16 bars.*

PICNIC LEMON BARS

¼ cup sifted confectioners' sugar
½ cup margarine, softened
1 cup self-rising flour
2 eggs, beaten
1 cup sugar
Grated rind of 1 lemon
2 tbsp. lemon juice
2 tbsp. self-rising flour

Cream together confectioners' sugar and margarine. Add 1 cup flour. Press into a greased 9-inch square baking pan. Bake in a 350-degree oven for 18 to 20 minutes. Remove from oven and set aside. Combine next five ingredients. Pour over baked crust. Return to oven and bake for 25 minutes longer. Cool. Cut into 2-inch bars. *Yields about 16 bars.*

PINK CLOUD DESSERT

1½ cups graham cracker crumbs
½ cup margarine, melted
½ cup sugar
1 8-oz. pkg. cream cheese, softened
1 1-lb. box sifted confectioners' sugar
1 3-oz. box strawberry gelatin
1½ cups boiling water
1 21-oz. can strawberry pie filling
1 12-oz. container whipped topping

Mix first three ingredients together. Press into a 13-by-9-inch pan. Bake in a 325-degree oven for 8 minutes. Remove from oven. Cool completely.

Mix together cream cheese and confectioners' sugar. Spread over cooled crust. Refrigerate. Dissolve gelatin in boiling water. Let cool in refrigerator for about 1 hour, until it begins to thicken but not set. Stir in strawberry pie filling. Spread over cream cheese layer. Refrigerate until set. Spread with whipped topping. Keep refrigerated. *Yields 12 servings.*

STRAWBERRY CREPES

3 eggs
⅛ tsp. salt
1 tsp. sugar
1½ cups all-purpose flour
1½ cups milk
2 tbsp. vegetable oil
Nonstick cooking spray
1 8-oz. pkg. cream cheese, softened
1¼ cups sifted confectioners' sugar
1 tbsp. lemon juice
1 tsp. grated lemon rind
½ tsp. vanilla
1 cup heavy cream, whipped
3½ cups sliced strawberries

In a mixing bowl, beat eggs. Add salt and sugar. Add flour alternately with milk, beating until smooth. Beat in oil. Spray an 8-inch skillet with nonstick cooking spray. Pour in 2 to 3 tablespoons batter in hot skillet. Tilt skillet until crêpe no longer runs. Turn to brown on both sides, then remove from pan. Repeat process until batter runs out. Stack between waxed paper. Cool.

Beat together cream cheese, sugar, lemon juice, rind, and vanilla. Fold in whipped cream and strawberries. Fill crêpes with about ⅓ cup of mixture. Roll up. Top each with any remaining cream mixture. *Yields 8 servings.*

QUICKIE APPLE OR PEACH COBBLER

    4 cups apples or peaches,
       peeled and chopped
    1 cup sugar
    ¼ tsp. salt
    ½ cup water
    1 box white or yellow cake mix
    ½ cup butter or margarine, melted

In a saucepan, mix together apples or peaches, sugar, salt, and water. Bring to a boil. Simmer for 15 minutes, stirring often to keep from sticking. Remove from heat. Pour half of fruit into a 9-by-9-inch square cake pan. Cover with half the cake mix and half the butter. Repeat with remaining fruit, cake mix, and butter. Bake in a 350-degree oven for 30 to 40 minutes, or until top is brown and mixture is bubbling. Serve warm with ice cream. *Yields 8 to 10 servings.*

VANILLA ICE CREAM

    4 eggs
    1 cup sugar
    1 14-oz. can sweetened condensed milk
    1 3½-oz. pkg. vanilla instant pudding
    2 tsp. vanilla
    1 qt. milk, plus additional milk to fill
       freezer bucket ⅔ full
    1-gallon ice cream freezer

Beat eggs thoroughly. Add sugar and beat until mixed well. Add sweetened condensed milk, pudding, and vanilla. Beat until smooth. Add 1 quart milk, stirring to mix well. Pour into ice cream bucket. Add enough milk to make two-thirds full, stirring to blend. Freeze. *Yields 1 gallon.*

STORIES

HEAD OF THE HOUSEHOLD?

The preacher's sermon was about marriage, the text being taken from Ephesians 5:23. He indicated the trouble with many marriages was the reluctance of the husbands to be head of the household as the Bible stated God intended them to be.

He told a story about a little man and his wife having a fight. The man crawled under the bed, and when the wife couldn't get to him, she got a broom and proceeded to punch him with the handle, trying to make him come out. She yelled, "You come out from under that bed, you little worm!" He shouted, "I'm head of this household, and I'll come out when I get good and ready."

A couple in the church seemed to fit this description perfectly. He was a little man of about 135 pounds, and she was near two hundred. When church dismissed and we went to our car, they were parked in front of us. She always did the driving, and as they approached the car, she was about to get in on the driver's side when he said, "I'll drive!" She said, "Why? I always do the driving." He repeated, "I said, I'll drive!" in a real forceful voice. She looked surprised, but got in the passenger's side anyway. He adjusted the seat and took off, spinning the wheels. I've often wondered if that little man got to sleep on the bed or under it that night.

COULD BE WORSE

One hot Sunday, the air conditioning went off in our church. People were fanning and complaining about being so hot. When the preacher got up to deliver his sermon, he pulled off his coat and said, "This ain't so bad. When I first started preaching, we didn't have air conditioning, and we didn't have deodorant either."

Miscellaneous and How-To

Followed by

I Know Not What the Truth May Be;
I'll tell These Tales as Told to Me

My niece, Cherry King, and her grandson Ty playing with play dough.

HELPFUL HINTS

• Wash and chop fresh herbs, and sprinkle over bottom of a cookie sheet. Place in freezer for an hour or so. Loosen with spatula and place in labeled airtight containers. Return to freezer. When ready to use, remove amount needed and return to freezer.

• Make dish rags out of old tablecloths; pot holders from unworn parts of old mattress covers or from boys' athletic socks. Make aprons out of old skirts and sheets, and everyday napkins from old towels or tablecloths.

• Vary your routine by using unmatched plates and other serving pieces that can be obtained very inexpensively at yard sales. Sarah Polk, the wife of our eleventh president, James K. Polk of Tennessee, had china featuring a variety of Tennessee wildflowers, so all dishes were different.

APPLE BUTTER

6 lb. apples
6 cups apple cider or apple juice
3 cups sugar
1 tsp. cinnamon
½ tsp. cloves

Core and quarter apples, but do not peel. Add cider or juice and cook in a large saucepan for 30 minutes, or until very soft. Remove from heat. Press through colander. Discard peel left in colander. Place apple pulp back into pan. Add sugar, cinnamon, and cloves. Cook over medium heat for about 1 hour, stirring often until desired thickness. Pour into 8 hot sterilized half-pint jars. Seal and process in hot water bath for 10 minutes. *Yields 8 half-pint jars.*

FREEZER PEACH JAM

2 cups fresh peaches, peeled, seeded and finely chopped
2 tbsp. lemon juice
4 cups sugar
¾ cup water
1 1¾-oz. pkg. powdered fruit pectin

Place peaches in blender to purée. Mix in lemon juice and sugar. Let stand 10 minutes. In a saucepan, combine water and fruit pectin. Bring to a boil and cook for 1 minute, stirring constantly. Remove from heat. Stir in peach mixture, stirring 3 minutes to mix well. Ladle into sterilized freezer jars, allowing ½-inch head space. Seal. Let stand at room temperature for 24 hours before placing in freezer. Keep any opened unfrozen jam refrigerated. *Yields 5 half-pint jars.*

FREEZER STRAWBERRY JAM

2 cups crushed strawberries
4 cups sugar
¾ cup water
1 1¾-oz. pkg. fruit pectin

Mix strawberries and sugar together. Let stand for 10 minutes, stirring often. In a saucepan, mix together water and fruit pectin. Bring to a boil and cook for 1 minute. Remove from heat. Stir into strawberries, stirring continuously for 3 minutes. Spoon into sterilized freezer jars, leaving ½-inch head space. Seal. Let stand at room temperature for 24 hours before placing in freezer. When opened, keep any unused jam refrigerated. *Yields 5 half-pint jars.*

CRANBERRY RELISH

4 cups fresh cranberries
2 cups sugar
½ cup water
½ cup orange juice
1 tsp. grated orange rind

Combine all ingredients in a heavy saucepan. Bring to a boil. Reduce heat and simmer for 10 minutes, stirring occasionally. Cool and pour into a covered container. Keep refrigerated. *Yields 1 pint.*

CHOCK'S GREEN TOMATO PICKLES

My brother Chock, who lives in Michigan, often had many tomatoes in his garden that had to be picked green before a frost. This is one way he made use of them.

> **18 lb. green tomatoes**
> **1 lb. onions**
> **3 pt. vinegar**
> **¼ cup salt**
> **5 cups sugar**
> **1¼-oz. pkg. pickling spice**

Wash and slice green tomatoes. Peel and slice onions. Mix together vinegar, salt, and sugar. Bring to a boil. Mix well. Add tomatoes and onions. Bring to a boil. Make a cloth bag and fill with ½ of a 1¼-oz. package of pickling spice. Drop bag in mixture. Boil briskly for 45 minutes, stirring often. Spoon into sterilized jars and seal. *Makes 9 to 10 quarts.*

BARBECUE SAUCE

This sauce is especially good for ribs or pork chops, cooked either on the grill or in the oven.

> **1 cup tomato ketchup**
> **1 tbsp. brown sugar**
> **1 tbsp. Worcestershire sauce**
> **1 tbsp. red wine vinegar**
> **⅛ tsp. cayenne pepper**
> **1 tbsp. soy sauce**

Blend all ingredients together in a saucepan. Place on heat and bring to a boil. Turn to simmer for about 3 minutes, stirring constantly. Remove from heat. *Yields 1 cup.*

ZUCCHINI RELISH

4 lb. zucchini squash
2 medium onions
2 bell peppers
2 tbsp. salt
2 cups sugar
1 cup white vinegar
1 cup water
1 tsp. celery seed
1 tsp. tumeric
½ tsp. nutmeg
¼ tsp. black pepper

In food processor using coarse blade, grind zucchini, onions, and bell peppers. Add salt and refrigerate overnight.

Rinse in cold water and drain well. In a large kettle, combine zucchini mixture and remaining ingredients. Bring to a boil. Turn heat down and boil gently for 10 minutes, stirring often. Remove from heat. Ladle into hot pint jars, leaving ½-inch head space. Seal and process in a hot water bath for 15 minutes. Start timing when water begins to boil. *Makes about 4 pints.*

LEMON MARINADE

½ cup oil
¼ cup lemon juice
2 tbsp. chopped green onion
1 clove garlic, minced
½ tsp. dried tarragon, crushed
¼ tsp. pepper

Combine all ingredients. Pour over meat. Cover and refrigerate for 6 hours or overnight, turning several times. Drain, reserving marinade. Cook meat as desired, brushing with marinade as it cooks. *Yields about 1 cup.*

PICKLED PEPPERS

About 2 lb. hot banana peppers
7 cups water
⅓ cup salt
1½ cups white vinegar
1 tbsp. dried crushed basil
1 tsp. dried crushed oregano
5 to 6 cloves garlic

Cut peppers open and remove seeds. Leave whole or, if peppers are large, cut into rings. Combine 4 cups water and salt. Pour over peppers and let stand overnight. Drain and rinse well. In a saucepan, combine 3 cups water, vinegar, basil, and oregano. Bring to a boil. Reduce heat and simmer for 10 minutes.

Pack peppers in half-pint jars, leaving ½-inch head space. Add 1 clove garlic to each jar. Pour hot liquid over peppers, wipe rims, and screw on lids. Process in boiling water bath for 10 minutes. Begin timing when water boils. Remove from water bath. Let set a day or two before serving. *Yields 5 to 6 half-pint jars.*

SWEET AND SOUR SAUCE

⅓ cup sugar
⅓ cup cider vinegar
¼ cup ketchup
2 tbsp. soy sauce
1 tbsp. cornstarch
½ cup pineapple juice

Combine first four ingredients in a small saucepan. Dissolve cornstarch in pineapple juice. Add to mixture in saucepan. Bring to a boil. Cook for 1 minute, or until thickened, stirring constantly. *Yields about 1 cup.*

HOW TO CLEAN AND COOK SHRIMP

Husk shrimp by breaking under shell and opening from front to back. Remove meat all in one piece. Remove dark vein from center back by making a shallow cut from end to end along the back. Rinse well. To cook, place shrimp in a saucepan. Cover with water, using 1 teaspoon salt for each quart of water. Boil 10 minutes. Drain. Use as is for Shrimp Cocktail or Shrimp Creole, or batter and fry.

DOG BISCUITS

2 cups all-purpose flour
1 cup shredded cheddar cheese
½ cup vegetable oil
4 to 5 tbsp. chicken or beef broth

Combine flour, cheese, and oil in a food processor until consistency of coarse meal. Slowly add broth while machine is running until mixture forms a ball. Roll out on lightly floured surface to ½-inch thickness. Cut in the shape of a bone. Place on an ungreased cookie sheet. Bake in a 400-degree oven for 10 to 15 minutes, until bottom of bones are brown. Cool. Store in zip-lock bags. Great snacks for your doggies. *Yields about 10 biscuits.*

PLAY DOUGH

This is a very inexpensive way to entertain kids. I made this for my grandchildren when they visited. I kept the play dough in sealed containers, and on their next visit six months later, it was still good. I didn't have to make another batch.

1 cup flour
½ cup salt
2 tsp. cream of tartar
1 cup water
1 tbsp. cooking oil
Food coloring

Combine flour, salt, and cream of tartar in a heavy saucepan. Stir in water and oil. Cook over medium heat, stirring constantly for about 3 minutes, or until mixture thickens and turns loose from sides of pan. Remove from heat. Add food coloring to desired shade. Let cool. Dough will remain soft and pliable as long as stored in an airtight container. *This makes enough to fill 2 eight-ounce containers.*

STORIES

NO USE CRYIN' OVER SPILT WHISKEY

"The sheriff and revenuers wuz really crackin' down on moonshinin' in these parts. The men in the county got to starvin' fer some whiskey, so they ordered up some from Jack Daniel's distillery.

"They was a comin' by my house with four jugs strapped to a ole mule. It was snow and ice on the ground. When they started down the hill in front of my house, the ole mule lost his footin' and fell, a throwin' them jugs to the ground. Well, them jugs started rollin' down the hill, a bumpin' into one another. The men went a runnin' after them jugs a slippin' and a slidin'. The jugs just kept on a rollin', stoppin' at the bottom of the hill and a bustin' to pieces. The whiskey wuz ah spillin' out on the snow, and them men wuz down on their knees a scoopin' up the snow in their hands and a suckin' on it. You shoulda seen it! It shore wuz a sight to behold!"

THE LONGHANDLES

Winter was approaching, so Papa went into town one Saturday morning to buy longhandled underwear for all us kids. Water was heating in the resevoir, and the wash tub was prepared in the kitchen by the cookstove for Saturday night baths. I got my bath, put on my new longhandles and went to bed.

The sheets on the beds were made of 26-inch unbleached domestic, so it was necessary to have a seam down the middle to make the sheets big enough for the bed. The seam served as a marker for each one's own side. When Hiram got his bath, put on his new longhandles, and went to get into his side of the bed next to the wall, he said, "Your foot's on my side. Move over or I'll kick you over!" I drew up my feet and gave him a big boost right in the stomach. He landed against the wall, the flap of his new drawers catching on a nail. For a few seconds, he just hung there; then the new drawers began to tear. When he fell down on the bed, the fight was on!

Mama heard the commotion, came in with a switch, and wailed us good. She said it didn't matter who started it, the new drawers were torn and we were both to blame. Hiram had to stay under the covers until Mama sewed up the tear in the new longhandles.

Index

A

A "Stupid" Mistake, 32
A Third Language, 111-12
Almond Cookies, 177
Ambrosia Cake, 131-32
Angel Food Cake, 132
Any Deterrent is Better than None, 30
Apples: Apple Butter, 207; Apple Butter Bread, 35; Apple Dapple Cake, 133; Apple Peach Betty, 189; Apple Rings, 189-90; Applesauce Cake, 134; Baked Apples-Fours with Hard Sauce, 191; Caramel Apples, 190; Fried Apples, 196; Quickie Apple or Peach Cobbler, 203
Attention Getter, 66

B

Baked Apples-Fours With Hard Sauce, 191
Bald Can Be Beautiful, 105
Bananas: Banana Bread, 35; Banana Nut Cake, 135; Banana Split Cake, 136; Fried Bananas, 197
Barbecue Sauce, 209
Basic White Sauce, 71
Be Careful—You may be a Fashion Setter, 65
Beans: Beans, Beans, Beans, 117; Green Bean Casserole, 122; Green Beans Amandine, 123; Hamburger Beans, 88; Red Beans and Rice, 93; Skillet Baked Beans, 125
Beef: Beans, Beans, Beans, 117; Beef and Rice Casserole, 71; Beef Stroganoff, 72; Beefy Corn Bake, 73; Dukles (Spaghetti and Meatballs), 83; Easy Meatball Stew, 85; Fried Steaks and Cream Gravy, 85; Good and Easy Chili, 86; Hamburger Beans, 88; Hamburger Macaroni and Cheese, 88; Mexican Lasagna, 89; Round Steak and Onion Gravy, 95; Salisbury Steaks and Gravy, 96; Sloppy Joes, 98; Sour Cream Meat Pies, 100; Spicy Meatballs, 21; Stuffed

Peppers, 101; Tacos, 102;
Zippy Cheese and Beef
Balls, 25
Black-Eyed Pea Salad, 55
Blushing Peaches, 191
Bon-Bons, 184
Breakfast Pizza, 74
Broccoli: Chicken and Broccoli
    Casserole, 76; Simple
    Steamed Broccoli, 125
Broiler Hot Dogs, 73
Brown Sugar Chess Pie, 162
Brunch Casserole, 74-75
Butter Cream Icing, 134
Butter Pecan Ice Cream Pie,
    163
Buttermilk Biscuits, 36
Butternut Bars, 192
Butternut Cake, 137
Bye-Bye Radar, 108-9

C

Cake Mix Bars, 192
Cakes: Ambrosia Cake, 131-
    32; Angel Food Cake, 132;
    Apple Dapple Cake, 133;
    Applesauce Cake, 134;
    Banana Nut Cake, 135;
    Banana Split Cake, 136;
    Butternut Cake, 137;
    Carrot-Pineapple-Coconut
    Cake, 138; Chocolate Ice
    Cream Cake, 139;
    Chocolate Syrup Cake, 140;
    Chocolate Upside-Down
    Cake, 141; Coconut Sour
    Cream Cake, 142; Cream
    Cheese Coffee Cake, 142-
    43; Cream Cheese Pound
    Cake, 143; Dirt Cake, 144;
    Easy Carrot Cake, 145;
    Fruit Cocktail Cake, 146;
    German Chocolate Cake,
    147; Lemon-Drop Cake,
    148; No-Bake Fruitcake,
    149; Orange Cake, 150;
    Orange Slice Cake, 151;
    Pear Cake, 152; Piña
    Colada Cake, 153;
    Pineapple Upside-Down
    Cake, 154; Pound Cake,
    155; Quick Red Velvet
    Cake, 156; Strawberry Jello
    Cake, 157; Triple Chocolate
    Cake, 157; Twinkie Cake,
    158; Vanilla Wafer Cake,
    158-59; Yogurt Pound
    Cake, 159
Caramel Apples, 190
Caramel Sauce, 193
Carrots: Carrot Pie, 164;
    Carrot Raisin Salad, 55;
    Carrot-Pineapple-Coconut
    Cake, 138; Copper Pen-
    nies, 118; Creamed Onions
    and Carrots, 117; Easy
    Carrot Cake, 145; Glazed
    Carrots, 121; Pickled Carrot
    Sticks, 123
Celery: Stuffed Celery, 22
Cheese and Bacon Omelet, 76
Cheese Tartlets, 15
Chef's Salad, 56
Cherries: Cherry Cheese Bars,
    194; Cherry Cream Cheese
    Pie, 164; Cherry
    Lemonade, 45

Chicken: Chicken and Broccoli Casserole, 76; Chicken and Rice in Tomato Sauce, 77; Chicken Gumbo, 77; Chicken in a Nest, 78; Chicken or Turkey à la King, 79; Chicken Parmesan, 78-79; Chili Chicken, 80; Deep-Fried Chicken Puffs, 17; Easy Chili Chicken, 84; Parmesan Chicken Bake, 90; Rice Krispies Chicken, 94; Tortilla Chicken, 100-101
Chili Chicken, 80
Chili Dogs, 80
Chock's Green Tomato Pickles, 209
Chocolate Cupcakes, 193
Chocolate Ice Cream Cake, 139
Chocolate Peanut Butter Bars, 194-95
Chocolate Sauce, 195
Chocolate Syrup Cake, 140
Chocolate Upside-Down Cake, 141
Citrus Crust, 160
Coconut Pecan Bars, 196
Coconut Pies, 165
Coconut Sour Cream Cake, 142
Complete Satisfaction, 67
Cookies: Almond Cookies, 177; Cream Cheese Cookies, 177; Crispy Oatmeals, 178; Danish Wedding Cookies, 178-79; Date Balls, 179; Graham Cracker Crisps, 180; Orange Refrigerator Cookies, 180-81; Peanut Butter Kiss Cookies, 181; Party Pastels, 182; Pecan Sandies, 183, Uncooked Fruit Roll, 183
Copper Pennies, 118
Corkscrew Salad, 56
Corn: Beefy Corn Bake, 73; Corny Dogs, 81; Cottage Cheese Corn Bread, 36; Racy Rice and Corn, 124
Corny Dogs, 81
Cottage Cheese Corn Bread, 36
Could Be Worse, 204
Cranberries: Cranberry Relish, 208; Glazed Pearl Onions and Cranberries, 122; Quick Cranberry Punch, 50
Cream Cheese Coffee Cake, 142-43
Cream Cheese Cookies, 177
Cream Cheese Dip, 15
Cream Cheese Pastry Shells, 160
Cream Cheese Pound Cake, 143
Creamed Onions and Carrots, 117
Creamy Noodles, 81
Crêpe Cups, 82
Crispy Oatmeals, 178
Crispy Tuna Balls, 16
Crock-Pot Potatoes, 118
Crusts: Citrus Crust, 160, Flaky Butter Crust, 161; Graham Cracker Crust, 161; Tart Crust, 162

INDEX • 217

Crusty Potato Balls, 119
Customs, 31

D

Daddies, Watch Your Step, 64
Danish Wedding Cookies, 178-79
Date Balls, 179
Deep Thoughts, 64
Deep-Fried Chicken Puffs, 17
Definitely a Generation Gap, 128
Dirt Cake, 144
Dog Biscuits, 212
Dog Bites, 16
Dressing for Fruit Salad, 57
Dukles (Spaghetti and Meatballs), 83

E

Easy Barbecued Pork, 84
Easy Boiled Custard, 45
Easy Carrot Cake, 145
Easy Cheesy Fudge, 184
Easy Chili Chicken, 84
Easy Meatball Stew, 85
Easy Potatoes Au Gratin, 119
Easy Sweet Biscuits, 37
Empty Pockets, 28
Enough Is Enough, 30
Everybody Needs Something To Look Forward To, 26-27

F

Fabulous Fudge, 185

False Kick Punch, 46
Fancy Fried Taters, 120
Fishing: The Fun Sport, 109-11
Flaky Butter Crust, 161
Freezer Peach Jam, 207
Freezer Strawberry Jam, 208
Fried Apples, 196
Fried Bananas, 197
Fried Onion Rings, 120
Fried Squash and Onions, 121
Fried Steaks and Cream Gravy, 85
Fruit Cocktail Cake, 146

G

German Chocolate Cake, 147
Ginger Bread, 37
Gingerade Punch, 47
Glazed Carrots, 121
Glazed Orange Bread, 38
Glazed Pearl Onions and Cranberries, 122
Good and Easy Chili, 86
Graham Cracker Crisps, 180
Graham Cracker Crust, 161
Grape Juice Crush, 48
Green and White Salad, 57
Green Bean Casserole, 122
Green Beans Amandine, 123
Green Onion Dip, 17
Green Pea Salad, 58

H

Half Off: Not Always a Bargain, 128
Ham and Cheese Logs, 18

Ham and Egg Rolls with Sour Cream Sauce, 18
Ham and Spinach Pie, 86-87
Ham, Potato, and Cheese Casserole, 87
Ham Salad in a Crust Bowl, 59
Hamburger Beans, 88
Hamburger Macaroni and Cheese, 88
Handcrafts: Just Not My Bottle Of Turpentine, 113-14
Head of the Household?, 204
Heavenly Fruit Pie, 165
Helpful Hints, 14, 34, 54, 70, 116, 130, 176, 206
Hillbilly Humor, 27
Hits Gonna be a Car, 28
Honey of a Dressing, 63
Hot Cocoa Mix, 47
Hot Fudge Sundae Dessert, 197
Hot Potato Salad, 58
How To Clean and Cook Shrimp, 212

I

Iced Tea, 48
Icing: Butter Cream Icing, 134
Is Your Gun Jammed?, 172
It Matters Not the Name, 174

J

Just Be Quiet!, 65
Just Stay Off the Tracks, 171

K

Key Lime Pie, 166

L

Layered Bars, 198
Lemons: Lemon Bread, 39; Lemon Cream Cheese Crescent Knots, 198; Lemon Icebox Pie, 167; Lemon Marinade, 210; Lemonade Pie 167; Lemon-Drop Cake, 148; Lemon-Lime Salad, 60; Picnic Lemon Bars, 201
Love Conquers All, 64

M

Macaroni and Cheese, 89
Machines Taking Over?, 112
Magic Cookie Bars, 199
Mexican Lasagna, 89
Microwave Peanut Brittle, 185
Mints, 186
Money Talks, 112
Mustard Potato Salad, 60
My Little Church in the Wildwood, 103-4

N

New Shoes? 28
No Left Turn, 105-6
No Use Cryin' Over Spilt Whiskey, 214
No-Bake Brownies, 199

No-Bake Fruitcake, 149
No-Sugar Punch, 49
No-Sugar Salad Dressing, 62
Not So "Well-Done," 174

O

Onions: Creamed Onions and Carrots, 117; Fried Onion Rings, 120; Fried Squash and Onions, 121; Glazed Pearl Onions and Cranberries, 122; Green Onion Dip, 17; Round Steak and Onion Gravy, 95
Orange Cake, 150
Orange Cottage Cheese Salad, 59
Orange Refrigerator Cookies, 180-81
Orange Sherbet Punch, 50
Orange Slice Cake, 151

P

Panhandler Egg Pie, 90
Parmesan Bread, 39
Parmesan Chicken Bake, 90
Party Pastels, 182
Pasta: Creamy Noodles, 81; Dukles (Spaghetti and Meatballs), 83; Hamburger Macaroni and Cheese, 88; Macaroni and Cheese, 89; Mexican Lasagna, 89; Quick Macaroni and Cheese, 94
Patio Punch, 49
Peaches: Blushing Peaches, 191; Apple Peach Betty, 189; Freezer Peach Jam, 207; Peachy Yam Bake, 200; Quickie Apple or Peach Cobbler, 203
Peanut Butter and Jelly Bars, 200
Peanut Butter Fudge, 187
Peanut Butter Kiss Cookies, 181
Pears: Pear Cake, 152; Pear Salad, 61
Peas: Black-Eyed Pea Salad, 55; Green Pea Salad 58; Split-Pea Soup, 62
Pecan Sandies, 183
People Helping People, 52
Peppers: Pickled Peppers, 211; Stuffed Peppers, 101
Pickled Carrot Sticks, 123
Pickled Peppers, 211
Picnic Lemon Bars, 201
Pies: Brown Sugar Chess Pie, 162; Butter Pecan Ice Cream Pie, 163; Carrot Pie, 164; Cherry Cream Cheese Pie, 164; Coconut Pies, 165; Heavenly Fruit Pie, 165; Key Lime Pie, 166; Lemon Icebox Pie, 167; Lemonade Pie 167; Pineapple Pie, 168; Plum Good Pie, 168; Pumpkin Pie, 169; Rhubarb Pie, 169; Sour Cream Meat Pies, 100; Vinegar Cobbler Pie, 170
Pimiento and Cheese Spread, 19
Piña Colada Cake, 153

Pineapples: Carrot-Pineapple-Coconut Cake, 138; Piña Colada Cake, 153; Pineapple Pie, 168; Pineapple Sherbet Punch, 50; Pineapple Upside-Down Cake, 154
Pink Cloud Dessert, 201
Pizza Casserole, 91
Pizza Toast, 19
Play dough, 213
Please Take Me Away, 103
Plum Good Pie, 168
Popeyes, 20
Popovers, 40
Pork: Breakfast Pizza, 74; Brunch Casserole, 74-75; Cheese and Bacon Omelet, 76; Cream Cheese Dip, 15; Easy Barbecued Pork, 84; Fancy Fried Taters, 120; Fried Steak and Cream Gravy, 85; Ham and Cheese Logs, 18; Ham and Egg Rolls with Sour Cream Sauce, 18; Ham and Spinach Pie, 86-87; Ham, Potato, and Cheese Casserole, 87; Ham Salad in a Crust Bowl, 59; Panhandler Egg Pie, 90; Pizza Casserole, 91; Pizza Toast, 19; Pork Chops and Potato Casserole, 91; Pork Sausage Dressing, 92; Potatoes Joann, 124; Potato-Ham Scallop, 93; Red Beans and Rice, 93; Sausage and Egg Tortillas with Cheese Sauce, 97; Sausage Pizza, 98; Sour Cream Sausage Strips, 20
Potatoes: Crock-Pot Potatoes, 118; Crusty Potato Balls, 119; Easy Potatoes Au Gratin, 119; Fancy Fried Taters, 120; Ham, Potato, and Cheese Casserole, 87; Hot Potato Salad, 58; Mustard Potato Salad, 60; Peachy Yam Bake, 200; Pork Chops and Potato Casserole, 91; Potatoes Joann, 124; Potato-Ham Scallop, 93
Pound Cake, 155
Pretzel Rolls, 41
Pronto Pups, 92
Pumpkin Pie, 169
Push-Button Defeat, 112-13

Q

Quick Cranberry Punch, 50
Quick Macaroni and Cheese, 94
Quick Red Velvet Cake, 156
Quick Yeast Rolls, 43
Quickie Apple or Peach Cobbler, 203

R

Racy Rice and Corn, 124
Red Beans and Rice, 93
Rhubarb Pie, 169

Rice: Beef and Rice Casserole, 71; Chicken and Rice in Tomato Sauce, 77; Racy Rice and Corn, 124; Red Beans and Rice, 93; Rice Krispies Chicken, 94; Spanish Rice, 99
Rolls or Bread, 42
Round Steak and Onion Gravy, 95

S

Sagging Memories, 106-7
Salisbury Steaks and Gravy, 96
Sauces: Barbecue Sauce, 209; Basic White Sauce, 71; Caramel Sauce, 193; Chocolate Sauce, 195; Sweet and Sour Sauce, 211
Sauerkraut and Wieners, 95
Sausage and Egg Tortillas with Cheese Sauce, 97
Sausage Pizza, 98
Shrimp Cocktail, 21
Shrimp Creole, 99
Sick Humor, 171
Simple Steamed Broccoli, 125
Skillet Baked Beans, 125
Sloppy Joes, 98
Sour Cream Meat Pies, 100
Sour Cream Sausage Strips, 20
Spanish Rice, 99
Spicy Hush Puppies, 40
Spicy Meatballs, 21
Spinach: Ham and Spinach Pie, 86-87; Spinach Casserole, 126; Spinach Salad, 61; Spinach Squares, 22
Split-Pea Soup, 62
Squash: Fried Squash and Onions, 121; Squash Dressing, 126
Strawberries: Freezer Strawberry Jam, 208; Strawberry Bread, 43; Strawberry Crêpes, 202; Strawberry Jello Cake, 157
Stuffed Celery, 22
Stuffed Cherry Tomatoes, 23
Stuffed Peppers, 101
Suckers, 188
Sweet and Sour Sauce, 211

T

Taco Squares, 24
Tacos, 102
Taken For Granted, 109
Tart Crust, 162
Tater Rolls, 44
That Ought to Do It, 67
The Captain's Fish Batter, 75
The Con Game, 30
The Country Store, 51-52
The Longhandles, 214
The Most Wonderful Surprise of All, 171-72
The Yard Sale, 31
Thousand Island Dressing, 63
Tiny Cheese Quiches, 24-25
Toasted Cheese Appetizers, 23
Tomatoes: Chock's Green Tomato Pickles, 209; Stuffed Cherry Tomatoes, 23

Too Cold For Comfort,
   31
Tortilla Chicken, 100-101
Triple Chocolate Cake, 157
Twinkie Cake, 158
Two-By-Two Fruit Salad, 63

U

Uncooked Fruit Roll, 183
Unselfish Love, 127

V

Vanilla Ice Cream, 203
Vanilla Wafer Cake,
   158-59
Veal Cutlets Parmesan, 102
Vinegar Cobbler Pie, 170

W

What a Sales Pitch!, 66
White Chocolate Fudge, 187
Who's Censoring Whom?,
   108
*Would You Have an Answer
   for this One?,* 65

Y

Yogurt Pound Cake, 159
You Can Have 'Em!, 173

Z

Zippy Cheese and Beef Balls,
   25
Zucchini Relish, 210